PROPHECY CHECKLIST

OVER ONE HUNDRED BIBLE PROPHECIES

COUNTING DOWN TO THE SECOND COMING

OF

JESUS CHRIST

by

James H. Warden Jr.

authorHOUSE®

AuthorHouse™
1663 Liberty Drive, Suite 200
Bloomington, IN 47403
www.authorhouse.com
Phone: 1-800-839-8640

First published by AuthorHouse 6/13/2008

ISBN: 978-1-4208-1801-7 (sc)

Printed in the United States of America
Bloomington, Indiana

This book is printed on acid-free paper.
Edited by Don & Carolyn Myers editors of
Good News Articles in New York Times

FOR ADDITIONAL COPIES CONTACT:
Book Order Hotline 1-888-280-7715
M-F 8am - 6pm EST

WWW.PROPHECYCHECKLIST.COM
WWW. HAVEYOUHEARDTHEGOODNEWS.ORG
E-MAIL <u>MINISTRYMAILNEWS@AOL.COM</u>

Digital Art Cover Designed by Ted Larson
home.earthlink.net/~theoson/Index.html

"Blessed is he that readeth, and they that hear the words of this prophecy, and keep those things which are written therein: for the time is at hand."

THE REVELATION 1:3
THE LAST BOOK OF THE BIBLE

This Book Is Dedicated to
Larry King of CNN And Others
Who Desire To Know
How It's All Going To End
And Have Eternal Life

ACKNOWLEDGMENTS

I thank my precious wife Opal whose interest in the book of Daniel and the last book in the Bible prompted her keen mind to ask me probing questions on this most intriguing subject. As we studied Daniel chapters 8 and 11, we were puzzled as to why none of the leading televangelists on the subject of prophecy were showing their audiences that America's war with the leaders of Iraq and Iran was predicted by Daniel long before America was discovered and Iraq and Iran were given their modern names. Therefore, to alert people of these prophecies that are rapidly coming to pass, I developed an abbreviated pictorial description of the end events at www. ProphecyChecklist.com. I wrote this book after viewing Barbara Walter's interview of Larry King on his 50th year in broadcasting. Miss Walters asked Mr. King if he could have two things what would he wish? Mr. King stated that what he wished he could not have. He proceeded to tell Miss Walters that he wished he could know how it was all going to end, and his second wish would be to have eternal life. His answers touched me, and I relayed them to my minister. My, then 95 year old pastor responded, "So, tell him! It's his Jewish right to know! He is Jewish, the Bible was written by Jewish men inspired by "the God of Israel" who wrote how it's all going to end! Jewish Scriptures screams eternal life, i.e. salvation, "is to the Jew first" and it is free to anyone who believes the report of their prophets." Hence, I dedicate this book to Larry King of CNN and all others who desire to know how it's all going to end and have eternal life. Though I wrote about this fascinating subject in high school essays, I never dreamed I would live in the generation that would actually see these events being fulfilled. I thank "the God of Israel" for His divine providence in the affairs of men. I also would like to honor the Jewish people who have suffered much in human history beginning in slavery in Africa. They were chosen of God to bring His Word into the earth by way of their scribes and prophets to inform the world how it's all going to end so that people could govern themselves accordingly. They were also chosen to bring forth the Savior of the World to rescue humanity from self-destruction. The compilation of these prophecies from the pens of Jewish writers of Holy Scripture pains me as I see their fulfillment approaching on the world's horizon. This book is my attempt to share their prophecies with you. To quote the last words spoken in a public address by Rev. Dr. Martin Luther King Jr. the night before his life was ended, "MINE EYES HAVE SEEN THE GLORY OF THE COMING OF THE LORD!" My prayer for you is the same as that of Elisha, the Jewish prophet of Israel, who prayed for his Israeli comrade while they both were surrounded by enemy forces, "LORD, I pray thee, open his eyes, that he may see."

> JAMES H. WARDEN JR.
> HAVE YOU HEARD THE GOOD NEWS

FOREWORD

This millennial age opened with airwaves and newspapers filled with shocking headlined events. Weather has become so tumultuous that it seems commonplace to hear of flooding, scores of tornadoes touching down in an evening, tsunamis, cyclones, and fierce hurricanes destroying coastal regions, and global record setting temperatures. The political climate is such that small nations are defying super powerful ones in detonating nuclear weapons against stern warnings. First world nations are now threatened by the seepage of nuclear arms into the hands of terrorists. This new millennial has witnessed the atomic scientists' Doomsday's Clock inch to within five minutes of midnight; the midnight of humanity's catastrophic destruction. The United States of America experienced its first Mid-East based terrorist attack, for her alliance with the nation of Israel, at the advent of the new millennia. Afterwards, the United States initiated an unprovoked attack on Iraq and later admitted its basis for the war proved groundless. The Middle East has become the epicenter of international turmoil with Israel's very existence being openly threatened by certain Arab states perplexing world leaders. The social landscape of the new millennia has changed with the gay rights movement's international acceptance and success among many European governments that recognize the rights of humans to live apart from the social norms and sexual mores of the Abrahamic based religions: Judaism, Christianity, and Islam. Israel has always had her enemies, but with ever increasing frequency, terrorism toward Israelis by suicide bombers in the name of God has turned peaceful shopping trips, wedding days, and ordinary bus rides in Israel into fearful sights of unspeakable carnage. This generation has seen blazed across the New York Times and heard over CNN airwaves of asteroids heading toward planet earth. Is all this coincidental? No. Thousands of years ago, Jewish prophets recorded that all these events, and more, would converge in the generation that would see Israel become a nation which occurred in May 1948. Prophecies heard in church are now seen on television, the west's war with Iraq's leader and its soon defeat of Iran's leader was predicted thousands of years before Christ by the Jewish prophet Daniel famed for his lion's den escape in Iraq, called Babylon in his time. It is the fourth quarter and the two minute warning is about to sound on the field of play. With the use of Jewish prophecies as a checklist, this book is a barometer of world events and conditions as it counts down to the end of this age as we know it.

Prophecy Checklist
Table of Contents

Section One Signs of the Last Days "The Beginning of Sorrows" 1

Section Two The West's War With the Leaders of Iraq and Iran as Prophesied by Daniel 9

Section Three The Tribulation Period Begins 17

Section Four Global Mass Destruction 25

Section Five The Seven Last Plagues 33

Section Six The Anti-Semite/Antichrist 39

Section SevenThe Coming of the Lord 77

Section EightThe Day of the Lord 87

Section NineJesus Christ's Millennial Reign................. 91

Section Ten Signs of His Second Coming.................... 107

Section Eleven The Biblical History of Iraq............... 121

Section Twelve The Prophetic Fulfillment of God's Timetable 125

Prophecy Finder Index.. 137

INTRODUCTION

PROPHECIES RECORDED IN JEWISH SCRIPTURES ARE NOW BROADCAST ON TELEVISION. THIS BOOK IS A COMPILATION OF JEWISH PROPHECIES FROM THE ANCIENT TEXTS OF THE OLD AND NEW TESTAMENTS. MOST AMERICANS HAVE IGNORED AND NEGLECTED THEIR BIBLES THAT ITS PROPHECIES ARE BEING FULLFILLED BEFORE THEM AND THEY DO NOT EVEN RECOGNIZE THEM. THIS BOOK SERVES ONLY AS A CHECKLIST OF THE ANCIENT JEWISH PROPHECIES FOR YOU TO NOTE THEM AS THEY OCCUR. THIS IS NOT A MENU OF THE ORDER OF THEIR EXECUTION AS THEY COME TO PASS.

JAMES H. WARDEN JR.
HAVE YOU HEARD THE GOOD NEWS

Section One

Signs of the Last Days "The Beginning of Sorrows"

Ground Zero
Israel to Become a Nation

"Thus saith the Lord GOD; I will even gather you from the people, and assemble you out of the countries where ye have been scattered, and I will give you the land of Israel."

(The Prophet Ezekiel 11:17)

"But, the LORD liveth, that brought up the children of Israel from the land of the north, and from all the lands whither he had driven them: and I will bring them again into their land that I gave unto their fathers."

(The Prophet Jeremiah 16:15)

"And I will return the captivity of my people Israel, and they shall build the waste cities and inhabit them; and they shall plant vineyards and drink the wine thereof; they also shall make gardens and eat the fruit of them. **AND I WILL PLANT THEM UPON THEIR LAND AND THEY SHALL NO MORE BE PULLED UP OUT**

1

OF THEIR LAND which I have given them, says the Lord thy God."

(The Prophet Amos 9:14-15)

"And it shall come to pass in that day, that the Lord shall set his hand again the second time to recover the remnant of his people... and he shall set up an ensign (a sign) for the nations, and shall assemble the outcasts of Israel and gather together the dispersed of Judah from the four corners of the earth... ."

(The Prophet Isaiah 11:11-13)

"Who hath heard such a thing? who hath seen such things? Shall the earth be made to bring forth in one day? or shall a **nation** be **born** at once? for as soon as Zion travailed [the Holocaust during World War II], she brought forth her children."

(Isaiah 66:8)

- This prophecy was fulfilled May 14, 1948

- WW II was the birth pangs of the nation of Israel

PROPHECY No. 1
TERRORISM TOWARDS ISRAELIS PREDICTED

The Apostle Paul wrote, "Know this that in the last days perilous times shall come." Jesus prophesied to the Jewish people in Israel that, "The time cometh, that whosoever killeth you will think that he doeth God service."

(1 Timothy 3:1-2, John 16:2)

✓ Suicide Bombings in Israel in The Name of God

PROPHECY No. 2
GREAT EARTHQUAKES & PANDEMICS PREDICTED

"Great earthquakes shall be in divers places, and famines, and pestilences [pandemic diseases]; and fearful sights."

(Jesus Christ: Luke 21:11)

GREAT EARTHQUAKES	=	HORRENDOUS NATURAL DISASTERS TO COME
FAMINES	=	ETHIOPIA, NIGER, SUDAN (MORE FOOD SHORTAGES TO COME)
PESTILENCE	=	MILLIONS OF PEOPLE DYING FROM PLAGUING DISEASES WORLDWIDE
FEARFUL SIGHTS	=	WORLD TRADE CENTER TOPPLING, BEHEADINGS (MORE FEARFUL SIGHTS TO COME)

PROPHECY No. 3
FIERCE HURRICANES PREDICTED

"And there shall be signs in the sun, and in the moon, and in the stars; and upon the earth distress of nations, with perplexity; the sea and the waves roaring [fierce hurricanes, typhoons, tidal waves and tsunamis]."

(Luke 21:25)

Weather is the earth's way of cooling itself, and with the rise of global temperatures, the earth's weather will become increasingly more violent as it attempts to cool itself, spawning horrendous hurricanes, treacherous tornadoes, and dramatic flooding.

PROPHECY No. 4
INFORMATION AGE PROPHESIED

"At the time of the end, many shall run to and fro and knowledge shall be increased."

(The Prophet Daniel 12:4)

- ✓ Invention of the Automobile & Aerospace travel
- ✓ Cloning & Bio-technology
- ✓ Medical advances
- ✓ Information Superhighway & Computer age
- ✓ More to Breakthroughs to come …

PROPHECY No. 5
CORPORATE GREED: THE RICH FRAUDULENTLY WITHHOLDING WAGES FROM LABORERS IN THE END TIMES

"Go now, **ye rich men**, weep and howl for your miseries that shall come upon you. Your riches are corrupted… Ye have heaped treasure together <u>for the last days</u>. Behold, the hire [money] of the labourers who have reaped down your fields, **which is of you kept back by fraud,** crieth: and the cries of them which have reaped are entered into the ears of the Lord… Ye have lived in pleasure on the earth, and been wanton; ye have nourished your hearts, as in a day of slaughter. Ye have condemned and killed the just [protesters]; and he doth not resist you. Be patient therefore, brethren, unto the coming of the Lord... Be ye also patient; stablish your hearts: <u>for the coming of the Lord draweth nigh</u>."

(James 5:1-8)

- ✓ Enron & WorldCom
- ✓ Tyco
- ✓ Adelphia
- ✓ Conseco
- ✓ Retirement Funds Raided by Fraud
- ✓ more fraud to come…

PROPHECY NO. 6
SUCCESSFUL GAY RIGHTS MOVEMENT
PREDICTED

"For as the lightning, that lighteneth out of the one part under heaven, shineth unto the other part under heaven; so shall also the Son of man be in his day....And as it was in the days of Noah [violence covered the earth and great floods worldwide], so shall it be also in the days of the Son of man… Likewise also as it was in the days of Lot…even thus shall it be in the day when the Son of man is revealed."

(Luke 17:24-30)

✓ Jesus stated that at His coming life will be not only as it was during the days of Noah but also as it was "in the days of Lot." (Luke 17:28) "Remember Lot's wife." (Luke 17:32) Both Lot and his wife lived in Sodom, a city legendarily famous for its homosexuality from "the old to the young." (Genesis 19:4) Sodom had degenerated to the point where men were gang-raping men during Abraham's time. (Genesis 19:5,8) Thus, Christ prophesied of a successful gay rights movement, "as it was in the days of Lot," that will encompass the globe prior to His Second Coming. (Jesus Christ—Luke 17:28-30, the story of Lot in Sodom is found in Genesis 19)

✓ These signs will not be exclusively to America but seen and noted worldwide.

✓ According to Genesis 19:14, when Lot tried to warn the inhabitants of Sodom of God's impending judgment, they thought he was mocking (joking), so shall it be for believers who attempt to warn the world of God's approaching judgment called the Tribulation Period also known as "the time of Jacob's [Israel's] trouble."(Jeremiah 30:7)

PROPHECY No. 7
JERUSALEM TO BECOME A MILLSTONE AROUND THE NECKS OF HER ALLIES

"Behold, I will make Jerusalem a cup of trembling unto all the people round about … And in that day will I make Jerusalem a burdensome stone for all people: all that burden themselves with it shall be cut in pieces, though all the people of the earth be gathered together against it."

(The Prophet Zechariah 12:2-3)

- ✓ **THE UNITED STATES REMAINS LOYALLY ALLIED WITH ISRAEL**

- ✓ **TERRORIST ATTACK ON AMERICAN SOIL (MORE TO COME)**

PROPHECY No. 8
THE GOSPEL OF THE KINGDOM IS SPREAD THROUGHOUT THE WORLD

"And this gospel of the kingdom shall be preached in all the world for a witness unto all nations; and then shall the end come."

(Matthew 24:14)

- ✓ Mel Gibson's movie "The Passion of the Christ" is available in every language.

Prophecy No. 9
The Second Coming of Jesus Christ is to be Mocked as Ridiculous in the Last Days

"Knowing this first, that there shall come <u>in the last days</u> scoffers, walking after their own lusts, and saying, Where is the promise of his coming? for since the fathers [Jewish fathers: *Abraham, Isaac, and Jacob*] fell asleep [died], all things continue as they were from the beginning of the creation."

(2 Peter 3:3-4)

"Enoch also, the seventh from Adam, prophesied of these, saying, Behold, the Lord cometh with ten thousands of his saints, To execute judgment upon all, and to convince all that are ungodly among them of all their ungodly deeds which they have ungodly committed, and of <u>all their hard speeches which ungodly sinners have spoken against him</u>."

(Jude 14,15)

- ✓ False claims such as Jesus bones found recently (more to come)

- ✓ False claims such as Jesus was married and had a love-child by Mary Magdalene

- ✓ Movies such as The Da Vinci Code, The Last Temptation of Christ, and Jesus Christ Superstar making a mockery of Christ

- ✓ Popular comedians openly mocking Jesus Christ, His message, the Rapture known in Scripture as "the blessed hope," and His Second Coming

- ✓ More hard speeches against Christ to come

SECTION TWO

THE WEST'S WAR WITH THE LEADERS OF IRAQ AND IRAN AS PROPHESIED BY DANIEL

PROPHECY NO. 10
THE WEST'S WAR WITH THE LEADERS OF IRAQ (MEDES) AND IRAN (PERSIA) AS PROPHESIED BY DANIEL

Iran and Iraq were once part of the Persian Empire. As a child the prophet Daniel, later famed for his "lion's den" experience, was kidnapped and taken to Babylon in ancient Persia's province now called Iraq. It was there that Daniel gave the interpretation of "the handwriting on the wall" and wrote the following prophecy regarding what is to befall Iraq and Iran in the last days. Daniel describes, in precise detail, how "at the time of the end," *a king of Media* [Iraq], described as one of two horns on a ram, would engage in expanding his territory "pushing westward, and northward, and southward," so that no one could withstand him and he would become great. (Daniel 8:4) The prophet wrote that these actions of this leader of the Medes (Iraqis) would stir the anger of a western king. (Daniel 8:5, 21) The leader proved to be Saddam Hussein who expanded his Iraqi kingdom in the early 90's which stirred the Ire of U.S. President George Herbert Walker Bush. Daniel prophesied that "at the time of the end" a ruler from western civilization, whom the prophet depicts as a stubborn male goat, would be "moved with choler" [unreasonable anger] that he will initiate an unprovoked attack on this Middle Eastern king and stomp him into the ground. (Daniel 8:7-20) It is very noteworthy that the king of the west will war against the kings of Media and Persia [Iraq and Iran] and not the people of their countries. Since the fulfillment of this prophecy, thus far, has been shared between two U. S. presidents, the office of U.S. presidency "at the time of the end" may represent "the king of the west."

According to Daniel's prophecy, after the king of the west destroys the king of the Medes [Iraq], the same western king will again initiate an attack on the second horn of the ram symbolizing the king of Persia (Iran), and stomp this leader into the dirt to the point that no nation could deliver either king out of his hand. After this rough he-goat king of the west defeats the kings of the Medes and the Persians, Iraq and Iran respectively, his nation will "wax [become] very great," and in the midst of its greatness its power shall be broken. (Dan. 8:8) Then, four nations will arise to fill the vacuum of world leadership. This is where Daniel prophesied of the rise of the greatest Anti-Semite/Antichrist he calls the *little horn*. (Dan. 8:9, 7:8) As we look on the world scene, we see the stage is being set before our eyes by the unseen hand of the Divine to bring this prophecy to pass. The major players in the last days will be Egypt, Israel, Iraq/Iran [also called Assyria/Babylon/Media/Persia] and the kings of the East, notably China. (Revelation 16:12) The following is the prophecy once fulfilled by Alexander the Great, but according to Daniel 8:17, 23 it will again serve as a pattern for the end times or "the time of the end." According to Daniel 8:27, this prophecy literally made the prophet sick, and it is very troubling to us who believe "the Scriptures of truth." (For a graphic pictorial description of the end times see www.prophecychecklist.com)

DANIEL 8

¹In the third year of the reign of King Belshazzar a vision appeared unto me, even unto me Daniel, after that which appeared unto me at the first. ²And I saw in a vision; and it came to pass, when I saw, that I was at Shushan in the palace, which is in the province of Elam; and I saw in a vision, and I was by the river of Ulai. ³Then I lifted up mine eyes, and saw, and, behold, there stood before the river **a ram which had two horns**: and the two horns were high; but one was higher than the other, and the higher came up last. **⁴I saw the ram pushing westward, and northward, and southward; so that no beasts might stand before him,** neither was there any that could deliver out of his hand; but he did according to his will, and became great. ⁵And as I was considering, behold, an **he goat came from the west** on the face of the whole earth, and touched not the ground: and the goat had a notable horn between his eyes. **⁶And he came to the ram that had two horns, which I had seen standing before the river, and ran unto him in the fury of his power.** ⁷And I saw him come close unto the ram, and **he was moved with choler against him, and smote the ram, and brake his two horns: and there was no power in the ram to stand before him, but he cast him down to the ground, and stamped upon him: and there was none that could deliver the ram out of his hand.** ⁸Therefore the **he goat waxed very great: and when he was strong, the great horn was broken;** and for it **came up four** notable ones **toward** the four winds of heaven. ⁹And **out of one of them** came forth **a little horn**, which waxed exceeding great, toward the south, and toward the east, and toward the pleasant land. ¹⁰And it waxed great, even to the host of heaven; and it cast down some of the host and of the stars to the ground, and stamped upon them. ¹¹Yea, he magnified himself even to the prince of the host, and by him the daily sacrifice was taken away, and the place of the sanctuary was cast down. ¹²And an host was given him against the daily sacrifice by reason of transgression, and it cast down the truth to the ground; and it practiced, and prospered. ¹³Then I heard one saint speaking, and another saint said unto that certain saint which spake, How long shall be the vision concerning the daily sacrifice, and the transgression of desolation, to give both the sanctuary and the host

to be trodden under foot? ¹⁴And he said unto me, Unto two thousand and three hundred days; then shall the sanctuary be cleansed. **¹⁵And it came to pass, when I, even I Daniel, had seen the vision, and sought for the meaning**, then, behold, there stood before me as the appearance of a man. ¹⁶And **I heard a man's voice between** the banks of Ulai, **which called, and said, Gabriel, make this man to understand the vision**. ¹⁷So he came near where I stood: and when he came, I was afraid, and fell upon my face: but he said unto me, Understand, O son of man: for **at the time of the end shall be the vision**. ¹⁸Now as he was speaking with me, I was in a deep sleep on my face toward the ground: but he touched me, and set me upright. ¹⁹And he said, Behold, **I will make thee know** what shall be in the last end of the indignation: for at the time appointed the end shall be. **²⁰The ram which thou sawest having two horns are the kings of Media [Iraq] and Persia [Iran]. ²¹And the rough goat is the king of Grecia [the seat of western civilization]: and the great horn [power] that is between his eyes is the first king.** ²²Now that being broken, whereas four stood up for it, four kingdoms shall stand up out of the nation, but not in his power. ²³And **in the latter time of their kingdom,** when the transgressors are come to the full, a king of fierce countenance, and understanding dark sentences, shall stand up [the Anti-Semite / Antichrist]. ²⁴And his power shall be mighty, but not by his own power: and he shall destroy wonderfully, and shall prosper, and practice, and shall destroy the mighty and the holy people. ²⁵And through his policy also he shall cause craft to prosper in his hand; and he shall magnify himself in his heart, and by peace shall destroy many: he shall also stand up against the Prince of princes [Jesus Christ the Son of God]; but he shall be broken without hand. ²⁶And the vision of the evening and the morning which was told is true: wherefore shut thou up the vision; for it shall be for many days. ²⁷And I Daniel fainted, and was sick certain days; afterward I rose up, and did the king's business; and I was astonished at the vision, but none understood it."

Daniel 8 KJV

This legend reveals Daniel's prophetic vision in our time:

HORNS	=	NATIONAL LEADERS POWER
RAM'S 1ST HORN / KING OF MEDIA (IRAQ) WHO ANGERS WESTERN KING	=	FORMER LEADER OF IRAQ SADDAM HUSSEIN
RAM'S 2ND HORN /KING OF PERSIA (IRAN)	=	LEADER MAHMOUD AHMADINAJAD
HE GOAT'S HORN (KING OF THE WEST)	=	**PRESIDENCY OF THE** UNITED STATES
THE LITTLE HORN, KING OF FIERCE COUNTENANCE	=	THE ANTI-SEMITE /ANTICHRIST
HE GOAT'S BODY	=	UNITED STATES OF AMERICA
THE RAM'S BODY	=	IRAQ AND IRAN
GABRIEL	=	ARCHANGEL
MIGHTY & HOLY PEOPLE	=	ISRAEL & BELIEVERS IN CHRIST

While in the Persian province which encompassed both Iran and Iraq, Daniel penned this ancient prophecy regarding what was to become of this region in the last days. Daniel prophesied that the West will destabilize this Middle East region by defeating the leaders of both Media (Iraq) and Persia (Iran) in this Medo-Persian Gulf region. The first portion of this prophecy was fulfilled by the western leader, George W. Bush, attack of Iraq's leader, Saddam Hussein, and as according to the prophecy, he now rest in the dust of the earth. At the writing of this book, we are looking forward to the fulfillment of the second half of this prophecy which is the leader or "king of the west" removal of the king of Persia (Iran) resulting in many years of Mid-east wars and rumors of wars. According to the prophecy, there shall be three leaders after the first king's, Saddam Hussein, violent removal by the west. Years later, his replacement will be removed in wartime not involving the west. (Daniel 11:19) The third leader will set about repairing the Persian Gulf's infrastructure and Daniel describes him as a "raiser of taxes," and in a short time into his reign will die of natural causes. (Daniel 11:20) Then a wonderful peacemaker, who will eventually show himself as the greatest Anti-Semite ever known, will enter the world stage with a peace plan for the Mid-East according to Daniel the prophet. (Daniel 11:21) Christians refer to this coming Mid-East peace leader as the Antichrist. (See Section Six: The Anti-Semite/ Antichrist)

HE'S GOT YOUR GOAT

The chief characteristic of a goat is its stubborn disposition toward irritations. It is no secret that President George W. Bush, from the great state of Texas, is not one who wavers, but is a stubbornly determined man. One need only to perform an internet search on words "George Bush" and "stubborn" to see myriads of professional articles written in regards this president's steadfast disposition. Throughout his presidency, President Bush's has uttered his motto which may become the insignia of his presidency, "We're going to stay the course."

It is of interest that the prophet Daniel refers to this western leader as a "he goat from the west." It is even more interesting how God subtly let the world know that President George W. Bush was to fulfill the role of the "he goat" "king of the west" in Daniel's prophecy. On the morning of September 11, 2001 while President George W. Bush was visiting an elementary school in Florida, he was alerted that terrorists had rammed planes into the World Trade Center twin towers in New York. This moment was captured on film for the world to see. President Bush was seated and reading a story to elementary school children. Filmmaker Michael Moore, in his film *Fahrenheit 911,* terribly ridiculed President Bush for remaining seated for what seemed to be an inordinate amount of time with a child's book in his hand after hearing the news of the attack on America at such a crucial point that was to impact the world. The filmmaker mercilessly made President Bush out to be a spectacle; however, it was the hand of God that directed this spectacle for the whole world to see. It was at that time that God gave the world a picture of who President George W. Bush was to model in Daniel's prophecy. The title of the story that President Bush was reading at the time he was alerted of the attack, was *My Pet Goat.* In the aftermath of what is called 9-11, President Bush, against world opinion, stubbornly initiated war against the King of the Medes (Iraq's Suddam Hussein) who did not have weapons of mass destruction as thought, yet he was put to death for his crimes against humanity. (Dan. 8:7, 20)

THE MAN WHO WOULD BE KING

In the year 2000, George W. Bush became President through one of the most controversial elections in American history. However, according to the book of Daniel, the prophet wrote, "Blessed be the name of God for ever and ever: for wisdom and might are his: And he changeth the times and the seasons: he removeth kings, and setteth up kings ...." (Dan. 2:20-21) Though it may be distasteful to some people, but according to these writings of the Prophet Daniel, rulers are set up by the Most High God, who rules in the kingdom of men. (Dan. 4:17) A former King of Iraq, Nebuchadnezzar, King of Babylon, decreed in the book of Daniel "that the most High ruleth in the kingdom of men, and giveth it to whomsoever he will, and [he] setteth up over it the basest of men." (Dan. 4:17)

King Solomon wrote, "The king's heart is in the hand of the LORD, as the rivers of water: he turneth it whithersoever he will." (Prov. 21:1) After destroying the king of the Medes, according to Daniel's prophecy, the king of western civilization will initiate another attack, this time against the leader of Persia (Iran) trouncing him to the ground. (Dan. 8:7, 20) Then the nation of the west will become great. (Dan. 8:8) In his attempt to establish democracy in the Medo-Persian Gulf region, President George W. Bush, unbeknownst to himself or his cabinet members, is fulfilling Bible prophecy as God's proverbial pet goat. According to Daniel's prophecy, President Bush will be successful in establishing an autonomous democracy in the Gulf region for the prophecy later reads that the actions of this western leader will eventually bring to power the Anti-Semite/Antichrist who will "obtain the kingdom by flatteries," i.e., a democratic campaign. (Dan. 11:21, 32) It is interesting that this "king of the west" who will accomplish these things is not just called a goat, known for having a stubborn disposition, but is called a "he goat" which means *male goat*. This may be indicative that a future leader of the west may be female. Unfortunately, the prophecy reads that, after the West becomes great, in the midst of its greatness the horn of its power shall be broken. Its superpower status will then shift to the oil rich nations of the Mid-East and to China. (Dan. 8:8, 21)

SECTION THREE

THE TRIBULATION PERIOD BEGINS

PROPHECY No. 11
THE TRIBULATION PERIOD BEGINS

"For then shall be great tribulation, such as was not since the beginning of the world to this time, no, nor ever shall be. And except those days be shortened [by His 2nd Coming], there should no flesh be saved: but for the elect's [Israel's] sake those days shall be shortened."

(Jesus Christ —Matthew 24:21-22)

- ✓ The Tribulation Period is called "the time of Jacob's [Israel's] trouble." (Jeremiah 30:7)

- ✓ The Tribulation Period will last approximately seven years.

- ✓ This period in time is also known as The Great Tribulation.

PROPHECY No. 12
JESUS CHRIST RELEASES THE FOUR HORSEMEN OF THE APOCALYPSE UPON THE EARTH

THE FIRST HORSEMAN: THE ANTI-SEMITE/ANTICHRIST

"When the Lamb opened one of the seals, I heard, as it were a noise of thunder… And I saw and behold a white horse: and he that sat on him had a bow: and a crown was given to him: and he went forth conquering, and to conquer."

(Revelation 6:2)

This horseman is the *Anti-Semite/Antichrist*; the coming global ruler of the world. (See Section Six entitled "The Anti-Semite / Antichrist")

PROPHECY No. 13
WAR IS UNLEASHED UPON THE EARTH

THE SECOND HORSEMAN: WAR

"And when he had opened the second seal there went out another horse that was red: and power was given to him that sat thereon to take peace from the earth, and that they should kill one another: and there was given to him a great sword." This red horse represents *war*.

(Revelation 6: 3-4)

PROPHECY NO. 14
WEAPONS OF MASS DESTRUCTION
UNLEASHED

"A noise shall come even to the ends of the earth [an explosion]; for the LORD hath a controversy with the nations, he will plead with …them. Behold, evil shall go forth from nation to nation [missiles launched], and a great whirlwind shall be raised up from the coasts of the earth [nuclear clouds]. And the slain of the LORD shall be at that day from one end of the earth even unto the other end of the earth [millions of people dead]: they shall not be lamented, neither gathered, nor buried; they shall be dung upon the ground."

(Jeremiah 25:31-33)

"And except those days should be shortened [by His 2nd Coming], there should no flesh be saved [alive upon the earth], but for the elect's sake [the Israelis' sake] those days shall be shortened:"

(Matthew 24:22)

PROPHECY NO. 15
NATIONAL LEADERS PERPLEXED

"And there shall be signs … upon the earth distress of nations, with perplexity…"

(Luke 21:25)

PROPHECY NO. 16
TERRORISM DISMANTLED AND THE WORDS FROM NATIONAL LEADERS PRIOR TO NUCLEAR DESTRUCTION

"For yourselves know perfectly that the day of the Lord so cometh as a thief in the night. <u>For when they shall say, Peace and safety; then sudden destruction</u> cometh upon them, as travail upon a woman with child; and they shall not escape. But ye, brethren, are not in darkness, that that day should overtake you as a thief."

(1 Thessalonians 5:2-4)

- ✓ "They have seduced my people, saying, Peace; and there was no peace." (Ezekiel 13:10)

- ✓ The announcement of "peace and safety" may be brought about when the major leaders of terrorist organizations are apprehended and terror cells disband. This could prove to be the detonation fuse of the "sudden destruction" that will impact the world.

- ✓ "Believe on the Lord Jesus Christ and thou shall be saved…" (Acts 16:31)

PROPHECY NO. 17
NUCLEAR CARNAGE

"And this shall be the plague wherewith the LORD will smite all the people that have fought against Jerusalem; Their flesh shall *consume away* while they stand upon their feet [before they hit the ground], and their eyes shall *consume away* in their holes, and their tongue shall *consume away* in their mouth."

(Zechariah 14:12)

Prophecy No. 18
Dust From Nuclear Blast Blocks Sunlight

"And it shall come to pass in that day, saith the Lord GOD, that I will cause the sun to go down at noon, and I will darken the earth in the clear day:"

(The Prophet Amos 8:9)

Prophecy No. 19
Radiation Produces Baldness on All Heads & Earth Mourns

"And I will turn your feasts into mourning, and all your songs into lamentation; and I will bring up sackcloth upon all loins, and baldness upon every head; and I will make it as the mourning of an only son, and the end thereof as a bitter day."

(Amos 8:10)

PROPHECY NO. 20
THE PLAGUE OF HAIL A
POSSIBLE NUCLEAR WINTER CAUSED BY
NUCLEAR WAR

"And there fell upon men a great hail out of heaven, every stone about the weight of a talent [58 lbs]: and men blasphemed God because of the plague of the hail; for the plague thereof was exceeding great."

(Revelation 16:21)

PROPHECY NO. 21
RADIATION MAKES CERTAIN LANDS
UNINHABITABLE

" For it is the day of the LORD's vengeance, and the year of recompenses for the controversy of Zion. And the streams thereof shall be turned into pitch, and the dust thereof into brimstone, and the land thereof shall become burning pitch. It shall not be quenched night nor day; the smoke thereof shall go up for ever: from generation to generation it shall lie waste; none shall pass through it for ever and ever."

(Isaiah 34:8-10)

"And it shall come to pass, when seventy years are accomplished, that I will punish the king of Babylon, and that nation, saith the LORD, for their iniquity, and the land of the Chaldeans, and will make it **perpetual desolations**."

(Jer. 25:12)

"For I have sworn by myself, saith the LORD, that Bozrah shall become a desolation, a reproach, a waste, and a curse; and all the cities thereof shall be **perpetual wastes**."

(Jer. 49:13)

"And the **land** of Egypt shall be desolate and waste; and they shall know that I am the LORD:… Behold, therefore I am against thee, and against thy rivers, and I will make the **land** of Egypt **utterly waste** and desolate, from the tower of Syene even unto the border of Ethiopia."

(Ezek. 29:9-10)

✓ The earth will last only 1,000 years after Christ's return; hence, the half life of radiation will prevent anyone from passing through its contaminated lands "for ever and ever."

PROPHECY NO. 22
THE MOST TERRIBLE FAMINE IN WORLD HISTORY

THE THIRD HORSEMAN: WORLD FAMINE

"…when he had opened the third seal… I beheld a black horse; and he that sat on him had a pair of balances in his hand. And I heard a voice in the midst of the four beasts say, A measure of wheat for a penny, and three measures of barley for a penny; and see that ye not hurt the oil or the wine." This horseman represents *famine* (food shortages).

(Revelation 6:5-6)

✓ CLIMATE CHANGE WILL CAUSE DROUGHT, CROP FAILURES, RESULTING IN FAMINE

✓ HONEY BEES THAT POLLINATE CROPS ARE DYING

✓ **WHEAT FARMERS ARE GROWING CORN TO FILL GAS CONSUMPTION NEEDS**

✓ **HUNGER RIOTS TO OCCUR**

PROPHECY NO. 23
MEN EATING THEIR OWN FLESH

"And he shall snatch on the right hand, and be hungry; and he shall eat on the left hand, and they shall not be satisfied: they shall eat every man the flesh of his own arm:"

(Isaiah 9:20)

PROPHECY NO. 24
NO ESCAPE FROM PESTILENCES, WAR OR FAMINE AND MONEY WILL BE WORTHLESS

"The sword is without [outside Jerusalem], and the pestilence and the famine within [inside Jerusalem]: he that is in the field shall die with the sword; and he that is in the city, famine and pestilence shall devour him. But they that escape of them shall escape, and shall be on the mountains like doves of the valleys, all of them mourning, every one for his iniquity. All hands shall be feeble, and all knees shall be weak as water. Horror shall cover them; and shame shall be upon all faces, and baldness upon all their heads [due to radiation]. They shall cast their silver in the streets, and their gold shall be removed: their silver and their gold shall not be able to deliver them in the day of the wrath of the LORD: they shall not satisfy their souls, neither fill their bowels…"

(Ezekiel 7:15-19)

Section Four

Global Mass Destruction

Prophecy No. 25
One Fourth of the World's Population is Killed

The Fourth Horseman: Death

"And when he had opened the fourth seal…I looked and behold a pale horse: and his name that sat on him was Death, and Hell followed with him. And power was given unto them over a fourth part [25 percent] of the earth, to kill them with sword, and with hunger, and with death…"

(Revelation 6:7-8)

✓ **8 billion people times 25% = 2 billion people dead**

PROPHECY NO. 26
ASTEROID HITS EARTH & DUST
TO BLOCK SUN

"And the fifth angel sounded, and I saw a star fall from heaven unto the earth: [an asteroid] and… the sun and the air were darkened…"

(Revelation 9:1-2)

✓ Many scientists believe this is how the Dinosaur Age ended.

PROPHECY NO. 27
ASTEROIDS SPRAY EARTH FOLLOWED BY A
GREAT EARTHQUAKE

"…When he had opened the sixth seal…And the stars of heaven fell unto the earth, [asteroids] even as a fig tree casteth her untimely figs, when she is shaken of a mighty wind…. there was a great earthquake; and the sun became black as sackcloth of hair, and the moon became as blood; …And the kings of the earth, and the great men, and the rich men, and the chief captains, and the mighty men, and every bondman [slave], and every free man, hid themselves in the dens and in the rocks of the mountains. And said to the mountains and rocks, Fall on us, and hide us from the face of him that sitteth on the throne, and from the wrath of the Lamb. For the great day of his wrath hath come; and who shall be able to stand?"

(Revelation 6:12-17)

✓ Per CNN and the *New York Times,* the earth is on near collision courses with asteroids in the years 2014, 2028, and 2029. For this cause, the United States space program has launched missions for the purpose of gathering information on such threatening asteroids. Our solar system may pass through a dangerous portion of our galaxy that may yield the "signs in the sun, and in the moon, and in the stars" that Christ spoke of, so get your telescopes ready. (Luke 21:25) Recall Jupiter was struck by a comet in 1994.

✓ Notice that slavery is prophesied to be active during the end times. CNN and the BBC are airing stories increasing in frequency of reports that slavery has revived in foreign lands such as in Africa, China, and India.

✓ Ironically, everyone on earth during this time will believe that Jesus the Christ, *the Passover Lamb of God*, is the one bringing these plagues upon all the inhabitants of the earth who refuse to accept His offering to be their Savior. They shall flee from Him, the wrath of the Lamb. (Revelation 6:16)

Prophecy No. 28
The Seventh Seal Opened

"When he [Jesus] had opened the seventh seal there was silence in heaven for a half an hour… then there was thunderings, lightnings, and an earthquake. And the seven angels with seven trumpets prepared themselves to sound."

(Revelation 8:1-6)

PROPHECY NO. 29
SEVEN TRUMPETS OF JUDGMENT SOUND AND EARTH'S ATMOSPHERE ATTACKS PLANT LIFE

"The first angel sounded, and there followed hail and fire mingled with blood, and they were cast upon the earth: and the third part of trees was burnt up, and all green grass was burnt up."

(Revelation 8:7)

PROPHECY NO. 30
ASTEROID FALLS INTO THE SEA AND ONE THIRD OF ALL SEA LIFE PERISHES

"And the second angel sounded, and as it were a great mountain burning with fire was cast into the sea [an asteroid]: and the third part of the sea became blood; And the third part of the creatures which were in the sea, and had life, died; and the third part of the ships were destroyed."

(Revelation 8:8-9)

✓ Many NASA space scientists, who will be able to see these prophesied events, work under a gag order on what information they can disclose to the general public.

PROPHECY NO. 31
ONE THIRD OF THE EARTH'S FRESH WATER SUPPLY IS CONTAMINATED

"And the third angel sounded, and there fell a great star from heaven, burning as it were a lamp, and it fell upon the third part of the rivers, and upon the fountains of waters; And the name of the star is called Wormwood: and the third part of the waters became wormwood; and many men died of the waters, because they were made bitter [contaminated]."

(Revelation 8:10-11)

✓ **Wormwood means bitter (Chernobyl in Russian)**

PROPHECY NO. 32
HEART ATTACKS BROUGHT ON BY FEAR

"Men's hearts failing them for fear, and for looking after those things which are coming on the earth: for the powers of heaven shall be shaken."

(Jesus Christ —Luke 21:26)

✓ **What's more fearful than watching an approaching asteroid(s) on a collision course with planet Earth after surviving previous Asteroid strikes?**

Prophecy No. 33
The Skies Are Darkened

"And the fourth angel sounded, and the third part of the sun was smitten, and the third part of the moon, and the third part of the stars; so as the third part of them was darkened, and the day shone not for a third part of it [eight hours], and the night likewise. And I beheld, and heard an angel flying through the midst of heaven, saying with a loud voice, Woe, woe, woe, to the inhabiters of the earth by reason of the other voices of the trumpet of the three angels, which are yet to sound!"

(Revelation 8:12-13)

Prophecy No. 34
Oxygen Supply Divinely Protected

"And the fifth angel sounded, and I saw a star fall from heaven unto the earth: [another asteroid] and ... the sun and the air were darkened by reason of the smoke ... And there came out of the smoke locusts upon the earth: and unto them was given power, as the scorpions of the earth have power. And it was commanded them that they should not hurt the grass of the earth, neither any green thing [our oxygen supplies], neither any tree; but only those men which have not the seal of God in their foreheads. And to them it was given that they should not kill them, but that they should be tormented five months: and their torment was as the torment of a scorpion, when he striketh a man. And in those days shall men seek death, and shall not find it; and shall desire to die, and death shall flee from them."

(Revelation 9:1-6)

PROPHECY NO. 35
NEW LOCUST LIFE FORMS EMERGE

"And the shapes of the locusts were like unto horses prepared unto battle; and on their heads were as it were crowns like gold, and their faces were as the faces of men. And they had hair as the hair of women, and their teeth were as the teeth of lions. And they had breastplates, as it were breastplates of iron; and the sound of their wings was as the sound of chariots of many horses running to battle. And they had tails like unto scorpions, and there were stings in their tails: and their power was to hurt men five months."

(Revelation 9:7-10)

✓ It is speculative but noteworthy that some believe that this may be a crude ancient description of manned green army helicopters firing bullets.

PROPHECY NO. 36
IRAQ ENTERS WORLD STAGE IN THE END TIMES WITH 200 MILLION MEN ARMY MARCHING ACROSS HER EUPHRATES RIVERBED

"And the sixth angel poured out his vial upon the great river Euphrates; and the water thereof was dried up, that the way of the kings of the east might be prepared.... One woe is past; and, behold, there come two woes more hereafter. And the sixth angel sounded, and I heard a voice ...which is before God, saying to the sixth angel which had the trumpet, Loose the four angels which are bound in the great river Euphrates. And the four angels were loosed, which were prepared for an hour, and a day, and a month, and a year, for to slay the third part of men [2.3 billion presently]. And the number of the army of the horsemen were two hundred thousand thousand

[200 million man army]: and I heard the number of them. By these three was the third part of men killed [1/3 of worlds population] by the fire, and by the smoke, and by the brimstone…"

(Revelation 16:12, 9:12-16,18)

PROPHECY NO. 37
WIDESPREAD DRUG ABUSE

"And the rest of the men which were not killed by these plagues yet repented not of the works of their hands, that they should not worship devils, and idols of gold, and silver, and brass, and stone, and of wood: which neither can see, nor hear, nor walk: Neither repented they of their murders, nor of their sorceries [translated from the Greek word: *pharmacia* i.e., drug abuse] nor of their fornication, nor of their thefts [looting]."

(Revelation 20:21)

- ✓ The Greek word translated sorceries was *pharmacia* from whence we get the word *pharmacy* in regards to drugs. Hence, they will not repent of their drug abuse.

- ✓ Notice all these plagues are centered in the East; in the orient where men still worship idols of gold, stone, and silver. The horn of the western power structure is destroyed according to Daniel Chapter 8 which will result in murders, drug abuse, and looting. This is none other than a primitive description of anarchy, the total breakdown of government.

Section Five

The Seven Last Plagues

Prophecy No. 38
The Seven Vials of The
Wrath of God Poured Upon Earth

"And I heard a great voice out of the temple [in heaven] saying to the seven angels, Go your ways, and pour out the vials of the wrath of God upon the earth. And the first went, and poured out his vial upon the earth; and there fell a noisome and grievous sore upon the men which had the mark of the beast [666 or his name], and upon them which worshipped his image." [See Section six: The Anti-Semite/Antichrist called the Beast in Scripture]

(Revelation 16:1-2)

Prophecy No. 39
Much Sea Life Destroyed

"And the second angel poured out his vial upon the sea; and it became as the blood of a dead man: and every living soul died in the sea."

(Revelation 16:3)

PROPHECY NO. 40
GLOBAL WARMING PEAKS

"And the fourth angel poured out his vial upon the sun; and power was given unto him to scorch men with fire. And men were scorched with great heat, and blasphemed the name of God, which hath power over these plagues: and they repented not to give him glory."

(Revelation 16:8-9)

✓ Notice that mankind will not acknowledge God as responsible for global warming peaking. Man will continue to give glory to pollution, greenhouse gases, cow flatulence, and etc rather than to Almighty God who has power over this plague. Men will with their gnawed tongues curse God's name rather than repent (turn away from) their ungodly deeds.

PROPHECY NO. 41
PAINFUL SORES & DARKNESS THROUGHOUT THE EARTH

"And the fifth angel poured out his vial upon the seat of the beast [the throne of the Anti-Semite / Antichrist]; and his kingdom was full of darkness; and they gnawed their tongues for pain. And blasphemed the God of heaven because of their pains and their sores, and repented not of their deeds."

(Revelation 16:10-11)

✓ Man is God's only creation that resists Him. Lion's cry to God for prey. (Ps. 104:21) Baby birds cry to God for their food. (Job 38:41) The sun and moon and "the sweet influences of Pleiades [a constellation]" obey God by staying in their assigned orbits. (Jer. 31:35-36, Job 38:31) The sea obeys His command for its waves come to the shore but not wash over the earth. (Jer. 5:22) Only man refuses to acknowledge or obey his Creator. As it is written, "The fool says in his heart, "*There is* no God." (Psalms 14:1) In the King James Version of the Bible italicized words were added by the translators to let the reader know that they were not in the original text but were added to assist the reader. Therefore, a more authentic rendering of this verse without its italicized word is: "The fool says in his heart, "No God."" Stark disobedience.

Prophecy No. 42
Armies of the East Summoned to Armageddon

"And the sixth angel poured out his vial upon the great river Euphrates [in Iraq]; and the water thereof was dried up, that the way of the kings of the east might be prepared [China etc]. For they are the spirits of devils, working miracles, which go forth unto the kings of the earth and of the whole world, to gather them to the battle of that great day of God Almighty. And he gathered them together into a place called in the Hebrew tongue Armageddon."

(Revelation 16:12-16)

✓ **Armageddon is an actual place. It is a vast serene valley located in Israel.**

PROPHECY NO. 44
THE GREATEST EARTHQUAKE IN WORLD HISTORY

"And the seventh angel poured out his vial into the air;… And there were voices, and thunders, and lightnings; and there was a great earthquake, such as was not since men were upon the earth, so mighty an earthquake, and so great…. And the cities of the nations fell."

(Revelation 16:17-19)

✓ "The earth shall reel to and fro like a drunkard." (Isaiah 24:20)

✓ "And they shall go into the holes of the rocks, and into the caves of the earth, for fear of the LORD… when he [God] ariseth to shake terribly the earth." (Isaiah 2:19)

PROPHECY NO. 45
SEVEN HORRORS YET TO BE REVEALED

"And I saw another mighty angel come down from heaven… and he set his right foot upon the sea, and his left foot on the earth, And cried with a loud voice, as when a lion roareth: and when he had cried, seven thunders uttered their voices. And when the seven thunders had uttered their voices, I was about to write: and I heard a voice from heaven saying unto me, Seal up those things which the seven thunders uttered, and write them not."

(Revelation 10:1-4)

Hence, there are seven other dreadful plagues that John was commanded not to write down.

1. _____

2. _____

3. _____

4. _____

5. _____

6. _____

7. _____

THE NEXT SECTION IS ABOUT THE "SUPERMAN" THAT THE WORLD AWAITS TODAY.   HE WILL SETTLE THE PRESENT MID-EAST CRISIS.   THE BIBLE REFERS TO HIM BY NAMES SUCH AS THE BEAST, THE MAN OF SIN, THAT WICKED, THE SON OF PERDITION (HELL), THE ASSYRIAN, THE LITTLE HORN, AND THE ANTICHRIST WHO WILL PROVE TO BE THE GREATEST ANTI-SEMITE WHO EVER LIVED AND HIS NUMBER IS SIX-SIX-SIX (666).

SECTION SIX

THE ANTI-SEMITE/ANTICHRIST

THE DESTABILIZATION OF PERSIA BY THE WEST

Until 1939, Persia was the name of what is now called Iraq. According to the eighth chapter of Daniel's prophecy, in the last days a king from the West, called a he goat, will be moved to attack the present day Persian Gulf provinces known as Iraq and Iran called Assyria, Babylon, Media, and Persia in ancient times. This western king will attack with "choler," meaning hostile anger, destabilizing the Persian Gulf region by stomping its kings to residue. (Daniel 8:3-5) Afterwards, several leaders will rise and fall in the Persian Gulf region. Then a leader referred to in Scripture as "the little horn" will not be given the kingdom at first, but will eventually obtain it "by flatteries [a democratic process], and by peace shall he destroy many." (Daniel 8:25, 11:21, 32) Americans can rest assured that President Bush will accomplish his aims in establishing democracy in the Gulf region. Prophets Jeremiah and Daniel wrote that a flattery elected politician of "fierce countenance" in the Mid-East will be a destroyer of "*the gentiles.*" (Jer. 4:7, Dan. 8:23) In the King James Version of the Bible the word "gentiles" was the term Moses, Christ, and Paul used in referencing Europeans, whose father was Noah's firstborn son, Japheth the Elder, father of the Caucasians. (Genesis 10:5, 21) Christ also referred to the Europeans of the Roman Empire as "the gentiles." (Mark 10:33-34) Paul was an apostle to the gentiles, i.e. the Europeans. Christ called the times in which we live "the time of the gentiles" in which Europeans will rule the world.

Unfortunately, at the end of European world-domination called "the times of the gentiles" in Scripture, a Middle Easterner referred to as "the Beast" is prophesied to be "a destroyer of the gentiles." (Jeremiah 4:7) America and Great Britain have stirred the proverbial pot of anti-European sentiments in the Arab world and gulf region. Therefore, Jeremiah's prophecy of "The destroyer of the gentiles is on his way" is no longer farfetched. For more information order Warden's <u>Complete Works of Blacks in the Bible and Prophecy of the Nations</u> from AuthorHouse at 1-888-280-7715.

PROPHECY No. 46
THE ANTI-SEMITE/ANTICHRIST WILL NOT KNOW HE IS THE ROD OF GOD'S ANGER

"O Assyrian [O Persian], the rod of mine anger, and the staff in their hand is mine indignation. I will send him against an hypocritical nation, and against the people of my wrath [the time of Jacob's (Israel's) trouble] will I give him a charge, to take the spoil, and to take the prey, and to tread them down like the mire of the streets. Howbeit <u>he meaneth not so, neither doth his heart think so; but it is in his heart to destroy and cut off nations not a few</u>."
(Isaiah 10:5-7)

✓ "The destroyer of the gentiles is on his way. He is gone forth from his place to make thy land desolate; and thy cities shall be laid waste, without inhabitant. For this gird you [yourself] with sackcloth, lament and howl: for the fierce anger of the LORD is not turned back from us." (Jeremiah 4:7-8)

PROPHECY NO. 47
THREE RULERS OF THE DESTABILIZED MIDDLE EAST REGION WILL COME TO POWER PRIOR TO THE RISE OF THE GREATEST ANTI-SEMITE EVER, KNOWN AS THE ANTICHRIST

"And now will I shew thee the truth. Behold, there shall stand up yet three kings in Persia [present day Iraq and Iran]; and the fourth shall be far richer than they all [the Anti-Semite / Antichrist]: and by his strength through his riches he shall stir up all against the realm of Grecia [Europe, and the king of the west]."

(Daniel 11:2)

PROPHECY NO. 48
THE FIRST OF PERSIAN GULF'S LAST FOUR RULERS
(SADDAM HUSSEIN)

"And a mighty king shall stand up, that shall rule with great dominion, and do according to his will. And when he shall stand up, his kingdom shall be broken, and shall be divided toward the four winds of heaven; and not to his posterity [his sons or daughters], nor according to his dominion which he ruled: for his kingdom shall be plucked up, even for others beside those."

(Daniel 11:3-4)

✓ Saddam Hussein's male posterity [sons, Uday and Qusay] were killed in war with the King of the West, neither did his surviving daughters inherit his throne.

PROPHECY No. 49
SECOND RULER OF PERSIAN GULF MARRIES A PRINCESS IN A PEACE AGREEMENT AND OFFSPRING TO WAGE WAR

"And the king of the south [Arabia] shall be strong, and one of his princes; and he shall be strong above him, and have dominion; his dominion shall be a great dominion. ⁶And <u>in the end of years</u> they shall join themselves together; for the king's daughter of the south shall come to the king of the north to make an agreement: but she shall not retain the power of the arm; neither shall he stand, nor his arm: but she shall be given up, and they that brought her, and he that begat her, and he that strengthened her in these times. ⁷But out of a branch of her roots shall one stand up in his estate, which shall come with an army, and shall enter into the fortress of the king of the north, and shall deal against them, and shall prevail:...and he shall continue more years than the king of the north."

(Daniel 11:5-8)

PROPHECY No. 50
ARABIAN RULERS SHALL WAR OVER GULF REGION

"So the king of the south shall come into his kingdom, and shall return into his own land. ¹⁰But his sons shall be stirred up, and shall assemble a multitude of great forces: and one shall certainly come, and overflow, and pass through: then shall he return, and be stirred up, even to his fortress. ¹¹And the king of the south shall be moved with choler, and shall come forth and fight with him, even with the king of the north: and he shall set forth a great multitude; but the multitude shall be given into his hand. ¹²And when he hath taken away the multitude, his heart shall be lifted up; and he shall cast down many ten thousands: but he shall not be strengthened by it."

(Daniel 11:9-12)

PROPHECY NO. 51
SECOND RULER OF GULF REGION
TO BE DEFEATED IN THE MIDST OF MANY
YEARS OF WAR

"For the king of the north shall return, and shall set forth a multitude greater than the former, and shall certainly come <u>after certain years</u> with a great army and with much riches. ¹⁴And in those times there shall many stand up against the king of the south: also the robbers of thy people shall exalt themselves to establish the vision; but they shall fall. ¹⁵So the king of the north shall come, and cast up a mount, and take the most fenced cities: and the arms of the south shall not withstand, neither his chosen people, neither shall there be any strength to withstand. ¹⁶But he that cometh against him shall do according to his own will, and none shall stand before him: and he shall stand in the glorious land, which by his hand shall be consumed. ¹⁷He shall also set his face to enter with the strength of his whole kingdom, and upright ones with him; thus shall he do: and he shall give him the daughter of women, corrupting her: but she shall not stand on his side, neither be for him. ¹⁸After this shall he turn his face unto the isles, and shall take many: but a prince for his own behalf shall cause the reproach offered by him to cease; without his own reproach he shall cause it to turn upon him. ¹⁹Then he shall turn his face toward the fort of his own land: but he shall stumble and fall, and not be found."

(Daniel 11:13-19)

✓ Notice that there will be a passage of many "years." This is why the Scriptures state that there shall be wars and rumor of wars, "but the end is not yet." (Matt. 24:6) We still have years ahead of us, but prophecies will continue being fulfilled albeit at a much slower pace.

Prophecy No. 52
Third Gulf Region Ruler Raises Taxes to Restore Its Infrastructure But Will Die of Natural Causes

The third ruler will "stand up in his estate a raiser of taxes in the glory of the kingdom, but within few days he shall be destroyed, neither in anger, nor in battle."

(Daniel 11:20)

✓ Taxes will be raised to repair the infrastructure destroyed by the west as well as to finance their army. This may indicate that the West will not finance the rebuilding of the Gulf's Region infrastructure.

Prophecy No. 53
The Belief System of the Anti-Semite/ Antichrist

"Neither shall he regard the God of his fathers, nor the desire of women, nor regard any god: for he shall magnify himself above all."

(Daniel 11:37)

✓ Whether he will be homosexual or just so committed to his aims is unknown, but his desire will not be toward women according to Daniel's prophecy.

✓ Although Christians refer to the coming of this greatest of Anti-Semites as the Antichrist, he will be against all religions; not regarding any god.

PROPHECY NO. 54
THE ANTI-SEMITE/ANTICHRIST HONORS A STRANGE GOD

Prior to his assassination, "Shall he honour the God of forces [a higher power]: and a god whom his fathers knew not shall he honour with gold, and silver, and with precious stones, and pleasant things. Thus shall he do ... with a strange god, whom he shall acknowledge and increase with glory..."

(Daniel 11:38-39)

PROPHECY NO. 55
THE ANTI-SEMITE/ANTICHRIST BRINGS PEACE COVENANT TO THE MIDDLE EAST

"...he shall magnify himself in his heart, and by peace shall destroy many."

(Daniel 8:25)

"And after the league [covenant] made with him he shall work deceitfully [betrayal]: for he shall come up, and shall become strong with a small people."

(Daniel 11:23)

"And through his policy also he shall cause craft to prosper in his hand..."

(Daniel 8:25)

✓ His policy of peace will begin by bringing peace to the Middle East beginning with Israel and the Arab states. The agreement (covenant of peace) will be that for seven years (a week as Daniel describes it), wherein Israel will agree not to invade Arab occupied territories, and for seven years the Arab nations will agree not to invade Israel.

PROPHECY NO. 56
SOLOMON'S TEMPLE TO BE REBUILT ON THE TEMPLE MOUNT

"But the court which is without the temple leave out, and measure it not; for it is given unto the Gentiles:…"

(Revelation 11:2)

✓ A Muslim house of worship called the Dome of the Rock is presently located on the Temple Mount in the area where the Court of the Gentiles was located in previous Jewish temple. Therefore, it will be permissible for this Muslim shrine to remain in this area when the Jewish temple is rebuilt.

✓ Orthodox Jews will reinitiate the daily animal sacrifices of lambs, bulls, goats, and doves in the rebuilt Jewish temple. (Daniel 9:27)

✓ The first 3 ½ years will be peaceful and world prosperity will reign, but in "the middle of the week" (3 ½ years) the Anti-Semite / Antichrist will break this covenant himself after his attempted assassination. (Daniel 9:27)

PROPHECY NO. 57
THE ASSASSINATION OF THE ANTI-SEMITE/ ANTICHRIST

The Apostle John referred to the Anti-Semite / Antichrist as "the beast," he prophesied "and I saw one of his heads as it were wounded to death; and his deadly wound was healed: and all the world wondered after the beast [the Anti-Semite / Antichrist]."

(Revelation 13:3)

✓ This is the Anti-Semite / Antichrist's mock resurrection of Jesus Christ. When he is "resurrected," he will break the covenant with Israel and go into the rebuilt temple and declare himself God, who has been raised from the dead. (1 Thessalonians 2:5)

✓ In keeping with history, any Arab leader who attempts to make peace with Israel is assassinated, i.e., Egypt's Anwar Sadat who attempted peace with Israel former Prime Minister Menachem Begin, and King Abdullah of Jordan who attempted peace with former Israeli Prime Minister Golda Meir. In the peace negotiations that were moderated by, then, President Bill Clinton, PLO President Yassar Arafat balked at an agreeable peace plan with Israeli Prime Minister Yitzhak Rabin possibly for this reason.

Prophecy No. 58
The Post-Raptured Pope of the Apostate Church Encourages Worship of Anti-Semite/Antichrist After His "Resurrection"

After the Anti-Semite / Antichrist's mock resurrection, a religious figure that the Scriptures call "the false prophet" will arise and occupy the position of Pope in the Catholic (Universal) Church that is left on earth after *the rapture* (See Prophecy No.150). He will "causeth the earth and them which dwell therein to worship the beast [the Anti-Semite / Antichrist] whose deadly wound was healed."

(Revelation 13:12)

Prophecy No. 59
The Post-Raptured Pope, Called "The False Prophet" Commands a Statue Be Made for the Anti-Semite/Antichrist after an Assassination Attempt

This exalted religious figure, the false prophet (post-raptured Pope), will "deceive them that dwell on the earth by the means of those miracles which he had power to do in the sight of the beast [the Anti-Semite / Antichrist]; saying to them that dwell on earth, **that they should make an image to the beast** [the Anti-Semite / Antichrist], which had the wound by a sword, and did live."

(Revelation 13:14)

✓ The "false prophet" who will occupy the position of Pope in the post-raptured church will be able to perform signs and wonders on behalf of the beast (Antichrist). This false prophet (post-raptured Pope) will deceive the inhabitants of the earth by ordering the world to set up an image in honor of the beast (the greatest Anti-Semite) who was wounded by the sword and yet lived.

✓ Since most European nations, champion an educated populous, will have been destroyed, it will not be difficult for these two leaders to have poor third world nations follow their economic and religious reforms.

PROPHECY No. 60
THE FALSE PROPHET COMMANDS ALL NATIONS TO WORSHIP THE STATUE OF THE ANTI-SEMITE/ ANTICHRIST OR BE EXECUTED

This (post-raptured Pope) "false prophet" from the post-raptured Catholic (Universal) Church will have "power to give life unto the image of the beast, that the image of the beast should both speak, and cause that as many as would not worship the image of the beast [the Anti-Semite / Antichrist's statue] should be killed."

(Revelation 13:15)

PROPHECY No. 61
THE FALSE PROPHET MANDATES THAT ALL PLEDGE ALLEGIANCE TO THE ANTI-SEMITE/ANTICHRIST BY TAKING THE "MARK"

The post-raptured Pope that the Scriptures refers to as "the false prophet" of the post-raptured Catholic Church will draft a policy that "causeth all, both small and great, rich and poor, free and bond, to receive a mark in their right hand, or in their foreheads: and that no man might buy or sell, save he that had the mark, or the name of the beast [the Anti-Semite / Antichrist], or the number of his name.... Let him that hath understanding count the number of the beast [the Anti-Semite / Antichrist]: for it is the name of a man; and his number is Six hundred (600) three score (3 x 20 = 60) and six (666)."

(Revelation 13:16-17)

✓ The Mark of the Beast, 666, or the name of the beast in the palm of one's hand or foreheads makes one *eligible* to be able to participate in the world's economic system. (Rev. 13:16-18)

✓ If a person takes the Mark of the Beast, the Anti-Semite / Antichrist's name, or 666 in one's right hand or forehead that person is *ineligible* to enter the kingdom of heaven, period.

✓ Tattooing is ever popular; so many people will not think it strange to receive a mark of 666 in their palm or forehead. Whether the mark will be a scar from an implanted chip or a bar-code on ones skin is unknown.

PROPHECY NO. 62
ALL THE ARMIES SURROUND JERUSALEM AND HER ENEMIES REJOICE

"And when ye shall see Jerusalem compassed [surrounded] with armies, then know that the desolation thereof is nigh. Then let them which are in Judaea [an area around Jerusalem] flee to the mountains; and let them which are in the midst of it depart out; and let not them that are in the countries enter thereinto. For these be the days of vengeance, that all things which are written may be fulfilled."

Jesus Christ: (Luke 21:20-22)

"All that pass by clap their hands at thee; they hiss and wag their head at the daughter of Jerusalem [the Jews], saying, Is this the city that men call The perfection of beauty, The joy of the whole earth? All thine enemies have opened their mouth against thee: they hiss and gnash the teeth: they say, We have swallowed her up: certainly this is the day that we looked for; we have found, we have seen it."

(Jeremiah's Lamentations 2:15-16)

✓ Arab nations will rejoice at the despair of the nation of Israel, when they see her on the brink of destruction, the day they dreamed of her annihilation.

PROPHECY No. 63

JEWS WARNED TO FLEE JERUSALEM WHEN THE ANTI-SEMITE/ANTICHRIST INVADES THEIR YET-TO-BE REBUILT JEWISH TEMPLE ON THE TEMPLE MOUNT

"When ye therefore shall see the abomination of desolation [the Anti-Semite / Antichrist], spoken of by Daniel the prophet, stand in the holy place [of Solomon's rebuilt temple]. Then let them which be in Judea [Israel] flee into the mountains: Let him which is on the housetop not come down to take any thing out of his house: Neither let him which is in the field return back to take his clothes. And woe unto them that are with child, and to them that give suck in those days! But pray ye that your flight [fleeing away] be not in the winter neither on the Sabbath day [Orthodox Jews do not work on the Sabbath]: For then shall be great tribulation, such as was not since the beginning of the world to this time, no, nor ever shall be. And except those days should be shortened [by His 2nd Coming], there should no flesh be saved: but for the elect's sake those days shall be shortened. Then if any man shall say unto you, Lo, here is Christ, or there; believe it not. For **there shall arise false Christs,**

and false prophets, and shall show great signs and wonders; insomuch that, if it were possible, they shall deceive the very elect. Behold, I have told you before. Wherefore if they say unto you, Behold he is in the desert; go not forth: behold, he is in the secret chambers; believe it not. For as the lighting cometh out of the east, and shineth even unto the west; so shall also the coming of the Son of man be."

(Jesus Christ: Matthew 24:15-27)

- ✓ Jesus Christ warned future generations of this global leader's invasion of their Jewish temple in Jerusalem.

- ✓ Here Christ is referring to Daniel's prophecy of the desecration of Jerusalem's temple when the Anti-Semite / Antichrist confiscates and occupies the rebuilt temple of Solomon, in Jerusalem, for 3½ years.

- ✓ The curious Christ seekers will be massacred for seeking Christ instead of being devoted to the Anti-Semite / Antichrist; therefore, Christ warns them not to go seeking for Him on earth. When Jesus Christ returns, the whole world will see Him. (Revelation 1:7)

PROPHECY NO. 64
THE ANTI-SEMITE/ANTICHRIST ENTERS THE ISRAELIS' TEMPLE STATING HE IS GOD

"Let no man deceive you by any means: for that day shall not come, except there come a falling away first, and that man of sin be revealed, the son of perdition [hell] who opposeth and exalteth himself above all that is called God, or that is worshipped, so that he as God sitteth in the temple of God, showing himself that he is God. Remember ye not, that, when I was yet with you, I told you these things? And now ye know what withholdeth [restrains] that he might be revealed in his time. And then shall that Wicked be revealed ... Even him, whose coming is after the working of Satan with all power and signs and lying wonders, And with all deceivableness of unrighteousness in them that perish; because they received not the love of the truth, that they might be saved. And for this cause God shall send them strong delusion [this mock resurrection, great signs, and wonders by the post raptured false prophet], that they should believe a lie: That they all might be damned who believe not the truth, but had pleasure in unrighteous."

(2 Thessalonians 2:3-12)

✓ The love of the truth they reject is found in John 3:16 that: "God so loved the world, that he gave his only begotten Son, that whosoever believeth in him should not perish, but have everlasting life." (Jesus Christ: John 3:16)

✓ "I am come in my Father's name, and ye receive me not: if another shall come in his own name [the Beast / the Antichrist], him ye will receive." (Jesus Christ: John 5:43)

PROPHECY NO. 65
THE TEMPLE IS DEFILED BY THE ANTI-SEMITE/ ANTICHRIST

"Yea, he magnified himself even to the prince of the host [Jesus the Christ], and by him the daily sacrifice was taken away, and the place of the sanctuary was cast down. And an host was given him against the daily sacrifice by reason of transgression, and it cast down the truth to the ground; and it practised, and prospered. Then I heard one saint speaking, and another saint said unto that certain saint which spake, How long shall be the vision concerning the [temple's] daily sacrifice, and the transgression of desolation, to give both the sanctuary and the host to be trodden under foot? And he said unto me, Unto two thousand and three hundred days [3½ years]; then shall the sanctuary be cleansed [at the 2nd Coming of the Savior, Jesus Christ]"… "when he [Jesus Christ] will thoroughly purge his floor [the area called the court of the gentiles on which the Dome of the Rock, a holy Islamic mosque sits]."

(Daniel 8:11-14, Matthew 3:12)

Prophecy No. 66
The Anti-Semite/Antichrist Curses God Almighty After Declaring Himself to be God

The Anti-Semite/Antichrist "shall do according to his will; and he shall exalt himself, and magnify himself above every god, and shall speak marvelous things against the God of gods, and shall prosper till the indignation be accomplished: for that that is determined shall be done."

(Daniel 11:36)

- ✓ The Anti-Semite/Antichrist's blasphemy toward the God of gods will resonate with people of the world who will hate God for bringing such harsh judgments upon the earth and allowing the nuclear war, famine, mass destruction, and pestilence on unbelieving men, women, and their children alike.

- ✓ Although Christians call him the Antichrist, the Bible states that he will magnify himself "above all that is called god," not just Jesus Christ and Allah, but idols too.

- ✓ We see America becoming more and more "anti-Christ" especially during the Christmas season. Traditional phrases such as Merry Christmas and Christmas Trees are being assaulted in overt attempts to expunge the name of "Christ" from American tradition. Traditional words such as Merry Christmas and Christmas Trees are being replaced by phrases like Happy Holidays, Season Greetings, and Xmas Trees indicative of a pro-antichrist atmosphere. The age of antichrist sentiments is settling upon the nation who once worshipped "the God of Israel," the God of the Bible that is referred to on American currency. In American history the United States' mantra was God and country. Yet, a telling sign of the times is displayed on the new millennium's American quarter with George Washington's back toward "In God We Trust" as his faces "Liberty." Soon the country's motto of "In God We Trust" will be expunged from American currency. A Psalmist wrote, "The wicked shall be turned into hell, and all nations that forget God." (Ps. 9:17) According to the Holy Scripture, we can see that America and other European nations that have also forgotten God are in for some hellish days ahead.

Prophecy No. 67
The Anti-Semite/Antichrist Curses the Raptured and Deceased Saints in Heaven

"And there was given unto him [the Anti-Semite / Antichrist] a mouth speaking great things and blasphemies; and power was given unto him to continue forty and two months [3 ½ years]. And he opened his mouth in blasphemy against God, to blaspheme his name, and his tabernacle, <u>and them that dwell in heaven</u> [raptured saints.]"

(Revelation 13:5-6)

PROPHECY NO. 68
THE ANTI-SEMITE/ANTICHRIST DECLARES WAR ON THE SAINTS OF GOD

"And it was given him [the Anti-Semite global ruler known as Antichrist] to make war with the saints, and to overcome them: and power was given him over all kindreds, and tongues, and nations. And all that dwell upon the earth shall worship him, whose names are not written in the book of life of the Lamb [Jesus] slain from the foundation of the world."

(Revelation 13:7-8)

✓ The definition of saints according to the Scriptures differs considerably from who the Roman Catholic Church qualifies as saints. According to Catholic tradition a person must be dead and then the Church of Rome must deem that person has performed a miracle in his or her lifetime and then that person is voted to become a saint. However, according to Scripture whosoever by faith accepts Jesus Christ as savior is counted as sanctified, holy, and declared righteous based on the merits of Jesus Christ's death, blood, and resurrection for their souls' salvation. Hence, they are declared "set apart," i.e., sanctified or a *saint* in the sight of God by the sacrifice of Jesus Christ and given the free gift of eternal redemption, eternal salvation, and eternal life, on the basis on what Christ did for them, and not what they did or do for Him (works). Salvation is a "free gift."

PROPHECY No. 69
THE ANTI-SEMITE/ANTICHRIST BLASPHEMES GOD AND CRUSHES BELIEVERS

"And he shall speak great words against the most High, and shall wear out the saints [believers in Christ during the Great Tribulation Period]."

(Daniel 7:25)

PROPHECY No. 70
THE ANTI-SEMITE/ANTICHRIST WILL BE REVERED

"And they worshipped the dragon [Satan] which gave power to the beast [Anti-Semite/Antichrist]: and they worshipped the beast [Anti-Semite/Antichrist]: saying, Who is like unto the beast? Who is able to make war with him?"

(Revelation 13:4)

PROPHECY No. 71
THE ANTI-SEMITE/ANTICHRIST GOES FORTH TO CONQUER

"He shall enter the glorious land and many countries shall be overthrown: but these shall escape out of his hand, even Edom, and Moab, and the chief of the children of Ammon [the Jordanians]."

(Daniel 11:41)

PROPHECY NO. 72
RUSSIA WARS AGAINST THE ANTI-SEMITE/ ANTICHRIST

"…He shall divide the land for gain [a price]. And at the time of the end shall the king of the South push at him and the king of the north [Russia] shall come against him like a whirlwind, with chariots, and with horsemen, and with many ships; and he shall enter into the countries, and shall overflow and pass over."

(Daniel 11:39-40)

PROPHECY NO. 73
THE ANTI-SEMITE/ANTICHRIST DEVASTATES EGYPT

"He shall stretch forth his hand also upon the countries and the land of Egypt shall not escape."

(Daniel 11:42)

✓ Egypt will be so devastated that neither man nor beast will be able to walk across its land for 40 years. (Ezekiel 29:10-11)

PROPHECY No. 74
THE ANTI-SEMITE/ANTICHRIST ENJOYS THE SPOILS OF WAR AND PRACTICES SOCIALISM THE REDISTRIBUTION OF WEALTH

"But he shall have power over the treasures of gold and silver, and over all the precious things of Egypt: and the Libyans and the Ethiopians shall be at his steps."

(Daniel 11:43)

"He shall enter peaceably even upon the fattest places of the province; and <u>he shall do that which his fathers have not done, nor his fathers' fathers; he shall scatter among them the prey, and spoil, and riches</u>: yea, and he shall forecast his devices against the strong holds, even for a time."

(Daniel 11:24)

PROPHECY No. 75
THE PEACE COVENANT WITH ISRAEL IS BROKEN

The Anti-Semite/Antichrist attacks Israel, "He hath put forth his hands against such as be at peace with him: <u>he hath broken his covenant.</u> "The words of his mouth were smoother than butter, but war was in his heart: his words were softer than oil, yet were they drawn swords."

(Psalms 55:20-21)

Prophecy No. 76
Jerusalem Is Invaded

"The kings of the earth, and all the inhabitants of the world, would not have believed that the adversary and the enemy should have entered into the gates of Jerusalem."

(Lamentations 4:12)

"And the Lord spake by his prophets saying…, thus saith the Lord God of Israel, Behold, I am bringing such evil upon Jerusalem and Judah, that whosoever heareth of it, both of his ears will tingle…. and I will forsake the remnant of mine inheritance [the nation of Israel] and deliver them into the hands of their enemies, Because they have done that which was evil in my sight, and have provoked me to anger, since the day their fathers came out of the land of Egypt, even until this day."

(2 Kings 21:16)

✓ In Jerusalem, the Israelites begged to shed the blood of an innocent man, the Son of God, of whom Pilate asked, "Why, what evil hath he done? But they cried out the more, saying, Let him be crucified. When Pilate saw that he could prevail nothing, but that rather a tumult was made, he took water, and washed his hands before the multitude, saying, I am innocent of the blood of this just person: see ye to it. <u>Then answered all the people, and said, His blood be on us, and on our children</u>." (Matthew 27:23-25)

✓ According to Jewish prophets, God will bring "such evil" on Jerusalem in this is "the time of Jacob's [Israel's] trouble."

PROPHECY NO. 77
A DIVIDED JERUSALEM TO BE PLUNDERED

"For I will gather all nations against Jerusalem to battle; and the city shall be taken, and the houses rifled, and the women ravished; and <u>half of the city</u> shall go forth into captivity, and the residue of the people shall not be cut off from the city."

(Zechariah 14:2)

"and the holy city [Jerusalem] shall they tread under foot forty and two months [3 ½ years]."

(Revelation 11:2)

✓ Recent U.S. Presidents want plans in the works to divide Jerusalem in half. This will eventually happen and ultimately result in this prophecy being fulfilled in that the Jewish "half of the city will go into captivity" with its "houses rifled and the women ravished," according to the Jewish prophet Zechariah.

PROPHECY NO. 78
JERUSALEM UNDER SIEGE BY THE ANTI-SEMITE/ANTICHRIST MAN-MADE FAMINE THAT SPAWNS CANNIBALISM WITHIN HER GATES

"But woe unto them that are with child, and to them that give suck, in those days! for there shall be great distress in the land, and wrath upon this people."

(Luke 21:23)

"And thou shalt eat the fruit of thine own body, the flesh of thy sons and of thy daughters, which the LORD thy God hath given thee, in the siege, and in the straitness, wherewith thine enemies shall distress thee: So that the man that is tender among you, and very delicate, his eye shall be evil toward his brother, and toward the wife of his bosom, and toward the remnant of his children which he shall leave: So that he will not give to any of them of the flesh of his children whom he shall eat: because he hath nothing left him in the siege, and in the straitness, wherewith thine enemies shall distress thee in all thy gates."

(Deuteronomy 28:53-55)

"Yea, all Israel have transgressed thy law, even by departing, that they might not obey thy voice; therefore the curse is poured upon us, and the oath that is written in the law of Moses the servant of God, because we have sinned against him. And he hath confirmed his words, which he spake against us, and against our judges that judged us, by bringing upon us a great evil: for under the whole heaven hath not been done as hath been done upon Jerusalem. As it is written in the law of Moses, all this evil is come upon us: yet made we not our prayer before the LORD our God, that we might turn from our iniquities, and understand thy truth. Therefore hath the LORD watched upon the evil, and brought it upon us: for the LORD our God is righteous in all his works which he doeth: for we obeyed not his voice."

(Daniel 9: 11-14)

✓ After this temple invasion, no food will be allowed in the Jewish half of Jerusalem causing a localized famine of barbaric proportions in this capital city.

✓ Per Moses' prophecy, those in the city of Jerusalem shall eat their young in the siege.

✓ "The tender and delicate woman among you, which would not adventure to set the sole of her foot upon the ground for delicateness and tenderness, her eye shall be evil toward the husband of her bosom, and toward her son, and toward her daughter, And toward her young one that cometh out from between her feet, and toward her children which she shall bear: for she shall eat them for want of all things secretly in the siege and straitness, wherewith thine enemy shall distress thee in thy gates." (Deuteronomy 28:56-57)

PROPHECY No. 79

TWO-THIRDS OF JEWS MASSACRED BY THE ANTI-SEMITE/ANTICHRIST, AS ISRAEL LOOKS IN VAIN FOR AMERICA TO RESCUE HER; ONLY ONE-THIRD OF THE JEWISH POPULATION IN THE LAND OF ISRAEL WILL SURVIVE

"And it shall come to pass, that in all the land, saith the LORD, two parts therein shall be cut off and die; but the third shall be left therein. And I will bring the third part through the fire, and will refine them as silver is refined, and will try them as gold is tried: they shall call on my name, and I will hear them: I will say, It is my people: and they shall say, The LORD is my God."

(Zechariah 13 :8-9)

"They that be slain with the sword are better than they that be slain with hunger: for these pine away, stricken through for want of the fruits of the field.... As for us, our eyes as yet failed for our vain help: in our watching we have watched for a nation that could not save us. They hunt our steps, that we cannot go in our streets: our end is near, our days are fulfilled; for our end is come. Our persecutors are swifter than the eagles of the heaven: they pursued us upon the mountains, they laid wait for us in the wilderness."

(Jeremiah's Lamentations 4:9, 17-19)

✓ "Who is able to make war against the beast [Anti-Semite/ Antichrist]?" (Revelation 13:4)

Prophecy No. 80
The World Is Astonished At the invasion of Israel and the Siege of Jerusalem

"The hands of the pitiful women have sodden [boiled] their own children: they were their meat in the destruction of the daughter of my people. The LORD hath accomplished his fury; he hath poured out his fierce anger, and hath kindled a fire in Zion, and it hath devoured the foundations thereof. The kings of the earth, and all the inhabitants of the world, would not have believed that the adversary and the enemy should have entered into the gates of Jerusalem."

(The weeping prophet of Israel's Lamentations 4:10-12)

✓ This is why "Jesus wept" over Jerusalem because He understood the prophecy that if the Israelis rejected Him as the Son of God, the Messiah of Israel, then according to their own prophets, the judgment of God for rejecting His Son would be that they would eat their own sons and daughters in the last days called the time of Jacob's trouble. (Jer.30:7)

Prophecy No. 81
The Anti-Semite/Antichrist is Called a Destroyer of the Gentiles (A Term For Europeans in Scripture)

"and the destroyer of the Gentiles is on his way; he is gone forth from his place to make thy land desolate; and thy cities shall be laid waste, without an inhabitant."

(Jeremiah 4:7)

✓ Before the resurrection of Jesus Christ, when the term Gentile was used in Scripture, it was always used in reference to Europeans.

✓ Moses referred to the descendants of Japheth, the father of the Caucasians as "the Gentiles." (Genesis 10:2-5)

✓ Christ referenced Europeans of Rome as "the Gentiles." (Mark 10:33)

✓ Paul the "Apostle to the Gentiles" preached exclusively to the Europeans. (Romans 11:13)

✓ The time prior to the rise of the Anti-Semite/Antichrist is referred to in Scripture as "*the times of the gentiles*," the era of European influence dominating world rule. (Luke 21:24)

✓ The only way cities of Europe will be "laid waste" without one inhabitant will be due to nuclear war.

PROPHECY No. 82
144,000 JEWISH MEN ORDAINED BY GOD TO PREACH THE GOSPEL OF THE KINGDOM DURING THE GREAT TRIBULATION

"Saying, Hurt not the earth, neither the sea, nor the trees, till we have sealed the servants of our God in their foreheads. And I heard the number of them which were sealed: and there were sealed an hundred and forty and four thousand of all the tribes of the children of Israel. Of the tribe of Judah were sealed twelve thousand. Of the tribe of Reuben were sealed twelve thousand. Of the tribe of Gad were sealed twelve thousand. Of the tribe of Aser were sealed twelve thousand. Of the tribe of Nephthalim were sealed twelve thousand. Of the tribe of Manasses were sealed twelve thousand. Of the tribe of Simeon were sealed twelve thousand. Of the tribe of Levi were sealed twelve thousand. Of the tribe of Issachar were sealed twelve thousand. Of the tribe of Zabulon were sealed twelve thousand. Of the tribe of Joseph were sealed twelve thousand. Of the tribe of Benjamin were sealed twelve thousand."

(Revelation 7:3-8)

✓ After believers in Christ for His eternal salvation are *raptured* from earth (see Prophecy No. 150), their gospel of the grace of God "to believe on the Lord Jesus Christ to be saved" will no longer be preached. According to John the Revelator, an angel will seal 144,000 virgin Jewish men, 12,000 from each of the allegedly lost twelve tribes of Israel to preach the gospel that John the Baptist preached, *"the gospel of the kingdom."* (Revelation 7:2-8)

✓ Unlike *the gospel of the grace of God* which states, "Believe on the Lord Jesus Christ and you will be saved," the message of *the gospel of the kingdom* is; "behold the Lamb of God that taketh away the sin of the world. Jesus who is called the Lamb is coming, make straight paths for his feet. Do not take the mark of the beast or the number of his name or his name in your palm or forehead, prepare your hearts for the coming of the Lord draweth nigh."

PROPHECY NO. 83
THE GOSPEL OF THE KINGDOM IS PREACHED TO ALL THE WORLD THEN SHALL THE END COME

"And this *gospel of the kingdom* will be preached in the whole world as a testimony to all nations, and then the end will come."

(Matthew. 24:14)

✓ "The end" culminates with the saints coming back with Jesus Christ at his Second Coming. Therefore, these saints will not be the ones preaching the gospel of the kingdom to all the earth. The gospel of the kingdom will be preached throughout the world by 144,000 sealed virgin Jewish men, who will be converted *after* the church is taken out of this world in what is known in Jewish Scripture as "the blessed hope" or "a mystery" but called *the rapture* of the church by gentile theologians, and then shall the end come.

Prophecy No. 84
God Commissions Two Witnesses to Earth

God will send two men to earth and they shall curse with plagues those with the mark of the beast, the beast's name, or 666 in their hand or forehead. John writes: "And I will give power unto my two witnesses, and they shall prophesy a thousand two hundred and threescore days [3½ years], clothed in sackcloth [black]... And if any man will hurt them, fire proceedeth out of their mouth, and devoureth their enemies: and if any man will hurt them, he must in this manner be killed. These have power to shut heaven, that it rain not in the days of their prophecy: and have power over waters to turn them to blood, and to smite the earth with all plagues, as often as they will.

"And when they shall have finished their testimony, the beast [the Anti-Semite/Antichrist] ... shall make war against them, and shall overcome them, and kill them."

(Revelation 11:3-7)

✓ Isn't it ironic that with all the sci-fi horror movies from Hollywood, not one film in the history of American cinema has attempted to dramatize the book of the Revelation and stay true to the Scriptures regarding the end times as recited in the Holy Scriptures and featured in this book.

Prophecy No. 85
Worldwide Media Covers the Deaths of the Two Witnesses

"And their dead bodies shall lie in the street of the great city [Jerusalem], which spiritually is called Sodom and Egypt, where also our Lord was crucified. And they of the people and kindreds and tongues and <u>nations shall see their dead bodies</u> [made possible by worldwide mass media outlets] three days and an half, and shall not suffer their dead bodies to be put in graves. And they that dwell upon the earth shall rejoice over them, and make merry, and shall send gifts one to another; because these two prophets tormented them that dwelt on the earth. And after three days and an half the spirit of life from God entered into them, and they stood upon their feet; and great fear fell upon them which saw them. And they heard a great voice from heaven saying unto them, Come up hither. And they ascended up to heaven in a cloud; and their enemies beheld [saw] them."

(Revelation 11:8-12)

✓ "And there was war in heaven: Michael and his angels fought against the dragon; and the dragon fought and his angels, ... And the great dragon was cast out, that old serpent, called the Devil, and Satan, which deceiveth the whole world: he was cast out into the earth, and his angels were cast out with him. Therefore rejoice, ye heavens, and ye that dwell in them... Woe to the inhabiters of the earth and of the sea! for the devil is come down unto you, having great wrath, because he knoweth that he hath but a short time." (Revelation 12:7-12)

Prophecy No. 86
Believers Will Be Betrayed to the State by Family Members

"…great signs shall be from heaven. But before all these, they shall lay their hands on you, and persecute you, delivering you up to the synagogues, and into prisons, being brought before kings and rulers for my name's sake. And it shall turn to you for a testimony. Settle it therefore in your hearts, not to meditate before what ye shall answer: For I will give you a mouth and wisdom, which all your adversaries shall not be able to gainsay nor resist.   And ye shall be betrayed both by parents, and brethren, and kinsfolks, and friends; and some of you shall they cause to be put to death. And ye shall be hated of all men for my name's sake."

(Jesus Christ: Luke 21:11-17)

Prophecy No. 87
The Anti-Semite/Antichrist Will Behead Preachers of the Gospel of Christ's Return, the Gospel of the Kingdom

"And I saw thrones, and they sat upon them, and judgment was given unto them: and I saw the souls of them that were <u>beheaded for the witness of Jesus,</u> and for the word of God, and which had not worshipped the beast, neither his image, neither had received his mark upon their foreheads, or in their hands; and they lived and reigned with Christ a thousand years."

(Revelation. 20:4)

Prophecy No. 88
The Anti-Semite/Antichrist Makes War Against God's Saints

The Anti-Semite/Antichrist, called the beast, and the little horn "made war with the saints and prevailed against them."

(Daniel 7:21)

Prophecy No. 89
God Avenges His Martyred Saints

"And the third angel poured out his vial upon the rivers and fountains of waters; and they became blood. And I heard the angel of the waters say, Thou art righteous, O Lord, which art, and wast, and shalt be, because thou hast judged thus. For they have shed the blood of saints and prophets, and thou hast given them blood to drink; for they are worthy. And I heard another out of the altar say, Even so, Lord God Almighty, true and righteous are thy judgments."

(Revelation 16:4-7)

Prophecy No. 90
Martyred Saints Receive White Robes From God

"…I saw under the altar [in heaven] the souls of them that were slain for the word of God, and for the testimony which they held: And they cried with a loud voice, saying, How long, O Lord, holy and true, dost thou not judge and avenge our blood on them that dwell on the earth? And white robes were given unto every one of them; and it was said unto them, that they should rest yet for a little season, until their fellowservants also and their brethren, that should be killed as they were, should be fulfilled."

(Revelation 6:9-11)

✓ The souls that will not submit to the reign of the Anti-Semite/ Antichrist in favor of Jesus Christ will be slain, by edict of the Anti-Semite/Antichrist, during the Great Tribulation which will be the last 3½ years of this Anti-Semite's seven year reign as ruler of the head (superpower) of all nations. Now, salvation is free just by placing one's faith in Jesus' death, blood, and resurrection for life everlasting coupled with the eternal forgiveness of sins. However, after the believers are taken out of this world, so this wicked one can be revealed, those who then choose to accept Jesus Christ as their salvation will pay for that decision, made under the reign of the Anti-Semite/Antichrist, with their lives. "Believe on the Lord Jesus Christ and thou shalt be saved."

PROPHECY No. 91
POST-RAPTURED CATHOLIC CHURCH OF ROME IS JUDGED

"Come hither; and I will show unto thee the judgment of the great whore that sitteth on many waters. With whom the kings of the earth have committed fornication, [she has had political influence with kings] and the inhabitants of the earth have been made drunk with the wine of her fornication [false doctrines]. And I saw the woman drunken with the blood of the saints, and with the blood of the martyrs of Jesus: [through inquisitions in the name of Christianity]...Here is the mind which hath wisdom. The seven heads are <u>the seven mountains on which the woman sits</u>. And the woman which thou sawest is <u>that great city, which reigned over the kings of the earth</u>."

(Revelation. 17:2-18)

✓ The church that believes in God and His Son Jesus Christ alone, for their soul's salvation is called the bride of Christ, a chaste virgin, whereas the false church that has political influence with kings and governments on the earth and has killed the saints in the name of Christianity is referenced to by St. John the Apostle "Mystery Babylon the Great Whore" according to Revelation 17:5-6. Furthermore, the Scripture above reveals her location is situated as a queen on the seven hills in Rome. Many born again Christians are in this church preaching the gospel of salvation through Jesus Christ.

✓ During the Middle Ages the Catholic Church in Rome, that sits on *"seven mountains,"* exercised great authority with and over the kings of the earth, whether it was by her Cardinals in France or her priests in Great Britain and elsewhere. Here God is bringing judgment on her for the blood of those martyrs that she shed in her earlier inquisitions. Today she is a shadow of her former self, but she shall rise in world prominence again.

✓ John's prophecy takes place after believers in Christ for salvation, including those in the Catholic Church, has been raptured out of this world. (See Prophecy No. 150). In John's vision of one of many beasts, he explains his vision of how God will have the Anti-Semite / Antichrist handle this post-raptured false church when a false prophet reigns from there who will turn the souls who missed the rapture hearts from seeking Jesus Christ to the worship of the Antichrist. John wrote, "And I saw the woman drunken with the blood of the saints, and with the blood of the martyrs of Jesus [by its inquisitions]: … And he saith unto me, The waters which thou sawest, where the whore sitteth, are peoples, and multitudes, and nations, and tongues. And the ten horns [Ten Middle

Eastern kings] which thou sawest upon the beast, these shall hate the whore [post-raptured false church], and shall make her desolate and naked, and shall eat her flesh, and burn her with fire. <u>For God hath put in their hearts to fulfill his will, and to agree, and give their kingdom unto the beast [Anti-Semite / Antichrist], until the words of God shall be fulfilled.</u> And the woman which thou sawest is that great city, which reigneth over the kings of the earth. And I heard another voice from heaven, saying, <u>Come out of her, my people, that ye be not partakers of her sins, and that ye receive not of her plagues. For her sins have reached unto heaven, and God hath remembered her iniquities.</u>" (Revelation 17:6 - 18:5)

PROPHECY NO. 92
THE ANTI-SEMITE/ANTICHRIST ATTACKS VATICAN CITY

"And I heard another voice from heaven, saying, Come out of her, my people, that ye be not partakers of her sins, and that ye receive not of her plagues. For her sins have reached unto heaven, and God hath remembered her iniquities…<u>Therefore shall her plagues come in one day, death, and mourning, and famine; and she shall be utterly burned with fire: for strong is the Lord God who judgeth her.</u> And the kings of the earth, who have committed fornication and lived deliciously with her, shall bewail her, and lament for her, when <u>they shall see the smoke of her burning,</u> Standing <u>afar off</u> for the fear of her torment, saying, Alas, alas that great city Babylon, that mighty city! <u>for in one hour is thy judgment come.</u> And the merchants of the earth shall weep and mourn over her; for no man buyeth their merchandise any more…The merchants of these things, which were made rich by her, shall stand <u>afar off</u> for the fear of her torment, weeping and wailing, <u>And saying, Alas, alas that great city, that was clothed in fine linen, and purple, and scarlet, and decked with</u>

gold, and precious stones, and pearls! For in one hour so great riches is come to nought. And every shipmaster, and all the company in ships, and sailors, and as many as trade by sea, stood <u>afar off, And cried when they saw the smoke of her burning, saying, What city is like unto this great city!</u> And they cast dust on their heads, and cried, weeping and wailing, saying, Alas, alas that great city, wherein were made rich all that had ships in the sea by reason of her costliness! <u>for in one hour is she made desolate. Rejoice over her, thou heaven, and ye holy apostles and prophets; for God hath avenged you on her</u>… And the light of a candle shall shine no more at all in thee; and the voice of the bridegroom and of the bride shall be heard no more at all in thee: for thy merchants were the great men of the earth; for by thy sorceries were all nations deceived. <u>And in her was found the blood of prophets, and of saints,</u> and of all that were slain upon the earth."

(Revelation 18:4-24)

- ✓ The Church of Rome has amassed such wealth that after the Anti-Semite / Antichrist declares himself God, he will demand this post-raptured Church to turn its wealth over to him and worship him, but she will refuse. Then the Anti-Semite / Antichrist, a Middle Easterner, will destroy this perceived post-raptured bastion of Christianity. According to the Apostle John, God will allow the Anti-Semite / Antichrist to execute his judgment on the Church of Rome and it will be blown off the map in less than an hour, according to Revelation 18:10. Today she is known as Vatican City.

- ✓ Due to nuclear radiation, all the merchants and kings of the earth will see "the smoke of her burning" will stand "afar off" lamenting her destruction.

Prophecy No. 93
The Stage is Set For the Great Battle of Armageddon

"And I saw an angel standing in the sun; and he cried with a loud voice, saying to all the fowls that fly in the midst of heaven, Come and gather yourselves together unto the supper of the great God; That ye may eat the flesh of kings, and the flesh of captains, and the flesh of mighty men, and the flesh of horses, and of them that sit on them, and the flesh of all men, both free and bond, both small and great."

(Revelation 19:17-18)

Section Seven

The Coming of the Lord

Prophecy No. 94
The Lord Assembles His Mighty Army to Invade Earth]

"Blow ye the trumpet in Zion, and sound an alarm in my holy mountain: let all the inhabitants of the land tremble: for the day of the LORD cometh, for it is nigh at hand; A day of darkness and of gloominess, a day of clouds and of thick darkness, as the morning spread upon the mountains: a great people and a strong; there hath not been ever the like, neither shall be any more after it, even to the years of many generations. A fire devoureth before them; and behind them a flame burneth: the land is as the garden of Eden before them, and behind them a desolate wilderness; yea, and nothing shall escape them. The appearance of them is as the appearance of horses; and as horsemen, so shall they run."

(The Prophet Joel 2:1-4)

Prophecy No. 95
Jesus Christ Returns

"And I saw heaven opened, and behold a white horse; and he that sat upon him was called Faithful and True, and in righteousness he doth judge and make war. His eyes were as a flame of fire, and on his head were many crowns; and he had a name written, that no man knew, but he himself. And he was clothed with a vesture dipped in blood: and his name is called <u>The Word of God</u>."

(Revelation 19:11-13)

"In the beginning was the Word and the Word was with God and the <u>Word was God</u>. And the Word was made flesh and dwelt among us…he was in the world and the world was made by him and the world knew him not."

(John 1:1,14,10)

Prophecy No. 96
The Second Coming of Jesus Christ

"And the armies which were in heaven followed him upon white horses, clothed in fine linen, white and clean. And he hath on his vesture and on his thigh a name written, KING OF KINGS, AND LORD OF LORDS."

(Revelation 19:14-16)

Prophecy No. 97
The Earth Laments Christ's Return

"Behold he cometh with clouds; and every eye shall see him, and they also which pierced him: and all kindreds of the earth shall wail because of him. Even so, Amen."

(Revelation 1:7)

PROPHECY NO. 98
ALL TRIBES OF THE EARTH MOURN CHRIST'S RETURN

"And then shall appear the sign of the Son of man in heaven: ...and then shall all the tribes of the earth mourn, and they shall see the Son of man coming in the clouds of heaven with power and great glory."

(Matthew 24:30, Revelation 18:4-24)

✓ The fulfillment of the prophecy of Christ's return was mentioned at His ascension into heaven on a cloud when men dressed in white said, "Ye men of Galilee, why stand ye gazing up into heaven? This same Jesus, which is taken up from you into heaven, shall so come in like manner as ye have seen him go into heaven." (Acts 1:9-11)

PROPHECY NO. 99
EVERY EYE ON EARTH SHALL SEE HIS SECOND COMING

"For as the lightning cometh out of the east, and shineth even unto the west; so shall also the coming of the Son of man be, and every eye shall see him."

(Matthew 24:27, Revelation 1:7)

PROPHECY NO. 100
KINGS OF THE EARTH MAKE WAR AGAINST CHRIST AT HIS RETURN

"And I saw the beast [the Anti-Semite / Antichrist], and the kings of the earth, and their armies, gathered together to make war against him that sat on the horse, <u>and</u> <u>against</u> <u>his</u> <u>army</u> [born again believers]."

(Revelation 19:19)

PROPHECY NO. 101
THE LORD TAKES VENGEANCE ON UNBELIEVERS

"...the Lord Jesus shall be revealed from heaven with his mighty angels, In flaming fire taking vengeance on them that know not God, and that obey not the gospel of our Lord Jesus Christ [to believe in Him for salvation]. Who shall be punished with everlasting destruction from the presence of the Lord, and from the glory of his power; When he shall come to be glorified in his saints, and to be admired in all them that believe in that day."

(2 Thessalonians 1:7-10)

PROPHECY NO. 102
THE BATTLE OF ARMAGEDDON CHRIST MASSACRES EARTH'S ARMIES

"...hearken, ye people: let the earth hear, and all that is therein; the world, and all things that come forth of it. For the indignation of the LORD is upon all nations, and his fury upon all their armies: he hath utterly destroyed them, he hath delivered them to the slaughter.

Their slain also shall be cast out, and their stink shall come up out of their carcasses, and the mountains shall be melted with their blood."

(Isaiah 34:1-3)

Prophecy No. 103
The Lord Will Fight for Jerusalem

"In that day shall the LORD defend the inhabitants of Jerusalem; and he that is feeble among them at that day shall be as David; and the house of David shall be as God, as the angel of the LORD before them. And it shall come to pass in that day, that I will seek to destroy all the nations that come against Jerusalem."

(Zechariah 12:8-9)

Prophecy No. 104
The Lord Destroys Those Who Fight Against Jerusalem

"And this shall be the plague wherewith the LORD will smite all the people that have have fought against Jerusalem; Their flesh shall consume away while they stand upon their feet [before they hit the ground], and their eyes shall consume away in their holes, and their tongue shall consume away in their mouth."

(Zechariah 14:12)

PROPHECY NO. 105
THE LORD UTTERS HIS MIGHTY VOICE BEFORE HIS ARMY, AND HIS SAINTS EXECUTE JUDGMENT

"Like the noise of chariots on the tops of mountains shall they leap, like the noise of a flame of fire that devoureth the stubble, as a strong people set in battle array. Before their face the people shall be much pained: all faces shall gather blackness [happens to exposed skin after an atomic blast]. They shall run like mighty men; they shall climb the wall like men of war; and they shall march every one on his ways, and they shall not break their ranks: Neither shall one thrust another; they shall walk every one in his path: and when they fall upon the sword, they shall not be wounded. They shall run to and fro in the city; they shall run upon the wall, they shall climb up upon the houses; they shall enter in at the windows like a thief. The earth shall quake before them; the heavens shall tremble: the sun and the moon shall be dark, and the stars shall withdraw their shining: And the LORD shall utter his voice before his army: for his camp is very great: for he is strong that executeth his word: for the day of the LORD is great and very terrible; and who can abide it?"

(Joel 2:5-11)

✓ Before Christ was crucified, He told Pilate that His kingdom was not of this world or else His servants would fight. (John 18:36) At His Second Coming, "when the kingdoms of this world become the kingdoms of the Lord and of his Christ," (Revelation 11:15) His servants [born again believers] will fight for Him.

"Let the saints be joyful in glory: let them sing aloud upon their beds. Let the high praises of God be in their mouth, and a two-edged sword in their hand; To execute vengeance upon the heathen, and punishments upon the people; To bind their kings with chains, and their nobles with fetters of iron; To execute upon them the judgment written: this honour have all his saints. Praise ye the LORD."

(Psalm 149:5-9)

PROPHECY No. 106
JESUS CHRIST SMITES THE NATIONS

"And the armies which were in heaven followed him upon white horses, clothed in fine linen, white and clean. And out of his mouth goeth a sharp sword, that with it he should smite the nations: and he shall rule them with a rod of iron: and he treadeth the winepress of the fierceness and wrath of Almighty God."

(Revelation 19:14-15)

✓ We do not know what the fierceness and wrath of Almighty God is because He has restrained Himself from it during our New Testament era called grace. He has restrained Himself so much so that many of today's intelligentsia do not believe He exists.

PROPHECY No. 107
CHRIST SLAYS THE ARMIES GATHERED AT ARMAGEDDON

"And the armies which were in heaven followed him... And the remnant were slain with the sword of him that sat upon the horse, which sword proceeded out of his mouth: and all the fowls were filled with their flesh."

(Revelation 19:14, 21)

PROPHECY NO. 108
THE BLOOD OF THE 200 MILLION MEN ARMIES, SLAIN BY CHRIST AT ARMAGEDDON, WILL BE MORE THAN THREE FEET DEEP AND COVER OVER 100 MILES

"And the winepress was trodden without [outside] the city [Jerusalem], and blood came out of the winepress, even unto the horse bridles, by the space of a thousand and six hundred furlongs [137 miles]."

(Revelation 14:20)

"I will leave thee upon the land, I will cast thee forth in the open field, and will cause the fowls of the heaven to remain upon thee, and I will fill the beasts of the whole earth with thee. I will lay thy flesh upon the mountains, and fill the valleys with thy height. I will also water with thy blood the land wherein thou swimmest, even to the mountains; and the rivers shall be full of thee."

(Ezekiel 32:4-6)

PROPHECY NO. 109
CHRIST PUTS DOWN THE ANTI-SEMITE/ ANTICHRIST & WATERS THE BATTLEFIELD WITH THE BLOOD OF EARTH'S ARMIES

"And the beast [the Anti-Semite/Antichrist] was taken, and with him the false prophet [post-raptured Pope] that wrought miracles before him, with which he deceived them that had received the mark of the beast, and them that worshipped his image. These both were cast alive into a lake of fire burning with brimstone. And the remnant were slain with the sword of him that sat upon the horse, which sword proceeded out of his mouth: and all the fowls were filled with their flesh."

(Revelation 19:20-21)

"And I will lay thy flesh upon the mountains, and fill the valleys with thy height. I will also water with thy blood the land wherein thou swimmest, even to the mountains; and the rivers shall be full of thee. And when I shall put thee out, I will cover the heaven, and make the stars thereof dark; I will cover the sun with a cloud, and the moon shall not give her light."

(Ezekiel 32:5-7)

PROPHECY No 110
THE ANTI-SEMITE/ANTICHRIST'S POWER IS BROKEN

"I will break the Assyrian [the Anti-Semite/Antichrist] in my land [Israel's valley of Armageddon], and upon my mountains tread him under foot: then shall his yoke depart from off them, and his burden depart from off their shoulders. This is the purpose that is purposed upon the whole earth: ...upon all the nations. For the LORD of hosts hath purposed, and who shall disannul it? and his hand is stretched out, and who shall turn it back?"

(Isaiah 14:25-27)

Section Eight

The Day of the Lord

Prophecy No. 111
The Kings of the Earth are Punished

"The earth shall reel to and fro like a drunkard, and shall be moved like a cottage; and the transgression thereof shall be heavy upon it; and it shall fall, and not rise again. And it shall come to pass in that day, that the LORD shall punish the host of the high ones that are on high, and the kings of the earth upon the earth. And they shall be gathered together, as prisoners are gathered in the pit, and shall be shut up in the prison [hell], and after many days shall they be visited [Judgment Day]. Then the moon shall be confounded, and the sun ashamed, when the LORD of hosts shall reign in mount Zion, and in Jerusalem, and before his ancients gloriously."

(Isaiah 24:20-23)

Prophecy No. 112
The Day of the Lord

"The great day of the LORD is near, it is near, and hasteth greatly, even the voice of the day of the LORD: the mighty man shall cry there bitterly. That day is a day of wrath, a day of trouble and distress, a day of wasteness and destruction, a day of darkness and gloominess, a day of clouds and thick darkness."

(Zephaniah 1:14-15)

PROPHECY NO. 113
CHRIST REVEALS THE WOUNDS FROM HIS CRUCIFIXION TO THE JEWISH SURVIVORS OF THE ANTI-SEMITE/ANTICHRIST'S SIEGE

"And one shall say unto him, What are these wounds in thine hands? Then he shall answer, Those with which I was wounded in the house of my friends."

(Zechariah 13:6)

- ✓ This will be the moment when the Jews realize their forefathers did indeed crucify their Messiah, as foretold by King David, Goliath's slayer, and a Jewish prophet from the perspective of Messiah in the Psalm immediately prior to the 23rd Psalm of "The Lord is my shepherd in Psalm 22." (Psalm 23:1)

- ✓ "They pierced my hands and my feet." (King David's prophecy in first person)

(Psalm 22:16, Luke 24:44)

PROPHECY NO. 114
JEWISH SURVIVORS OF THE TRIBULATION MOURN THE SINS OF THEIR FOREFATHERS' CRUCIFIXION OF JESUS CHRIST

"…and they shall look upon me whom they have pierced, and they shall mourn for him, as one mourneth for his only son, and shall be in bitterness for him, as one that is in bitterness for his firstborn."

(Zechariah 12:10)

SECTION NINE

JESUS CHRIST'S MILLENNIAL REIGN

PROPHECY NO. 115
THE MILLENNIAL (THOUSAND YEAR) REIGN OF JESUS CHRIST BEGINS

"And the seventh angel sounded; and there were great voices in heaven, saying, The kingdoms of this world are become the kingdoms of our Lord, and of his Christ; and he shall reign for ever and ever."

(Revelation 11:15)

✓ Nostradamus also predicted this thousand years of peace after the Great War. Yet, John, the Jewish Revelator, foretold this long before Nostradamus was born and read John's Revelation of Jesus Christ, the last book in the Bible. Ironically, secular society believes in the predictions of Nostradamus and virtually ignore and ridicule the prophecies of Scripture written by Jewish prophets thousands of years before Nostradamus' birth.

PROPHECY NO. 116
SATAN IS BOUND FOR A THOUSAND YEARS AND CAST INTO THE BOTTOMLESS PIT

"And He [Jesus Christ] laid hold on the dragon, that old serpent, which is the Devil, and Satan, and bound him a thousand years. And cast him into the bottomless pit, and shut him up, and set a seal upon him, that he should deceive the nations no more, till the thousand years should be fulfilled: and after that he must be loosed a little season."

(Revelation 20:2-3)

PROPHECY NO. 117
SATAN MOCKED BY WORLD LEADERS ALREADY IN HELL AS HE DESCENDS INTO ITS PIT

"Hell from beneath is moved for thee to meet thee at thy coming: it stirreth up the dead for thee, even all the chief ones of the earth; it hath raised up from their thrones all the kings of the nations. All they shall speak and say unto thee, Art thou also become weak as we? art thou become like unto us? Thy pomp is brought down to the grave, and the noise of thy viols: the worm is spread under thee, and the worms cover thee. How art thou fallen from heaven, O Lucifer, son of the morning! how art thou cut down to the ground, which didst weaken the nations!... Yet thou shalt be brought down to hell, to the sides of the pit. They that see thee shall narrowly look upon thee, and consider thee, saying, Is this the man that made the earth to tremble, that did shake kingdoms; That made the world as a wilderness, and destroyed the cities thereof; that opened not the house of his prisoners? All the kings of the nations, even all of them, lie in glory, every one in his own house. But thou art cast out of thy grave like an abominable branch, and as the raiment of those that are slain, thrust through with a sword, that go down to the stones of the pit; as a carcass trodden under feet. Thou shalt not be joined with them in burial, because thou hast destroyed thy land, and slain thy people: the seed of evildoers shall never be renowned."

(Isaiah 14:9-20)

✓ Beware of the New International Version Bible's discourse in Isaiah 14:12. The NIV Bible removes Satan's name "Lucifer" and inserts the title of *morning star,* a title which belongs exclusive to Jesus Christ. Christ is known as "the bright and morning star." (Revelation 22:16) The NIV translation of this verse leans toward an interpretation that may lead people to believe that Christ weakened the nations.

PROPHECY NO. 118
CHRIST ESTABLISHES JERUSALEM AS THE CAPITOL OF THE WORLD

"At that time they shall call Jerusalem the throne of the LORD; and all the nations shall be gathered unto it, to the name of the LORD, to Jerusalem..."

(Jeremiah 3:17)

PROPHECY No. 119
JERUSALEM FINALLY AT PEACE

The Lord will make Jerusalem live up to her name the city of Peace. "Whereas thou has been forsaken and hated, so that no man went through thee, I will make thee an eternal excellency, a joy of many generations. Thou shalt also suck the milk of the Gentiles, and shalt suck the breast of kings: and thou shalt know that I the LORD am thy Saviour and thy Redeemer, the mighty One of Jacob. For brass I will bring gold, and for iron I will bring silver, and for wood brass, and for stones iron: I will also make thy officers peace, and thine exactors righteousness. Violence shall no more be heard in thy land, wasting nor destruction within thy borders; but thou shalt call thy walls Salvation, and thy gates Praise."

(Isaiah 60:15-18)

PROPHECY No. 120
THE HOUSE OF THE LORD SHALL BE
ESTABLISHED

"But <u>in the last days</u> it shall come to pass, that the mountain of the house of the LORD shall be established in the top of the mountains, and it shall be exalted above the hills; and people shall flow unto it [the Temple Mount]. And many nations shall come, and say, Come, and let us go up to the mountain of the LORD, and to the house of the God of Jacob; and he will teach us of his ways, and we will walk in his paths: for the law shall go forth of Zion, and the word of the LORD from Jerusalem. And he shall judge among many people, and rebuke strong nations afar off…"

(The Prophet Micah 4:1-4)

✓ "And I will execute great vengeance upon them with furious rebukes; and they shall know that I am the LORD, when I shall lay my vengeance upon them." (Ezekiel 25:17)

PROPHECY NO. 121
CHRIST BRINGS TRUE PEACE TO THE MIDDLE EAST

In that day "…they shall beat their swords into plowshares, and their spears into pruning hooks: nation shall not lift up a sword against nation, neither shall they learn war any more. But they shall sit every man under his vine and under his fig tree; and none shall make them afraid: for the mouth of the LORD of hosts hath spoken it."

(Micah 4:3-4)

PROPHECY NO. 122
A HIGHWAY OUT OF EGYPT IS TO BE BUILT

"In that day shall there be a highway out of Egypt to Assyria [Persian Region], and the Assyrian [the Persian] shall come into Egypt, and the Egyptian into Assyria, and the Egyptians shall serve with the Assyrians. In that day shall Israel be the third with Egypt and with Assyria, even a blessing in the midst of the land: Whom the LORD of hosts shall bless, saying, Blessed be Egypt my people, and Assyria the work of my hands, and Israel mine inheritance."

(Isaiah 19:23-25)

Prophecy No. 123
Peace on Earth
The Lion Will Lie Down In Peace With The Lamb

"The wolf also shall dwell with the lamb, and the leopard shall lie down with the kid; and the calf and the young lion and the fatling together; and a little child shall lead them. And the cow and the bear shall feed; their young ones shall lie down together: and the lion shall eat straw like the ox. And the sucking child shall play on the hole of the asp, and the weaned child shall put his hand on the cockatrice' den. They shall not hurt nor destroy in all my holy mountain: for the earth shall be full of the knowledge of the LORD, as the waters cover the sea."

(Isaiah 11:6-9)

Prophecy No. 124
Israel To Be Comforted By Her King

"Rejoice ye with Jerusalem, and be glad with her, all ye that love her: rejoice for joy with her, all ye that mourn for her: That ye may suck, and be satisfied with the breasts of her consolations; that ye may milk out, and be delighted with the abundance of her glory. For thus saith the LORD, Behold, I will extend peace to her like a river, and the glory of the Gentiles like a flowing stream: then shall ye suck, ye shall be borne upon her sides, and be dandled upon her knees. As one whom his mother comforteth, so will I comfort you; and ye shall be comforted in Jerusalem. And when ye see this, your heart shall rejoice, and your bones shall flourish like an herb: and the hand of the LORD shall be known toward his servants, and his indignation toward his enemies."

(Isaiah 66:10-14)

✓ Christ will still have enemies on earth during His thousand year reign.

PROPHECY No. 125
JESUS CHRIST REIGNS IN JERUSALEM AS KING OF KINGS AND LORD OF LORDS

"Of the increase of his government and peace there shall be no end, upon the throne of David, and upon his kingdom, to order it, and to establish it with judgment and with justice from henceforth even for ever. The zeal of the LORD of hosts will perform this…And in mercy shall the throne be established: and he shall sit upon it in truth in the tabernacle of David, judging, and seeking judgment, and hasting righteousness."

(Isaiah 9:7, 16:5)

PROPHECY No. 126
THE ORIGINAL TWELVE APOSTLES ARE INSTALLED AS JUDGES OVER ISRAEL

"And Jesus said unto his disciples, Verily [truly] I say unto you, That ye which have followed me, in the regeneration when the Son of man shall sit in the throne of his glory, ye also shall sit upon twelve thrones, judging the twelve tribes of Israel."

(Matthew 19:28)

PROPHECY No.127
CHRIST ANNEXES VAST AMOUNTS OF LAND IN THE MID-EAST AS NEW ISRAEL TO FULFILL GOD'S OLD TESTAMENT PROMISE TO, HIS CHOSEN PEOPLE, THE JEWS

"Every place whereon the soles of your feet shall tread shall be yours: from the wilderness and Lebanon, from the river, the river Euphrates, even unto the uttermost sea shall your coast be."

(Deuteronomy 11:24)

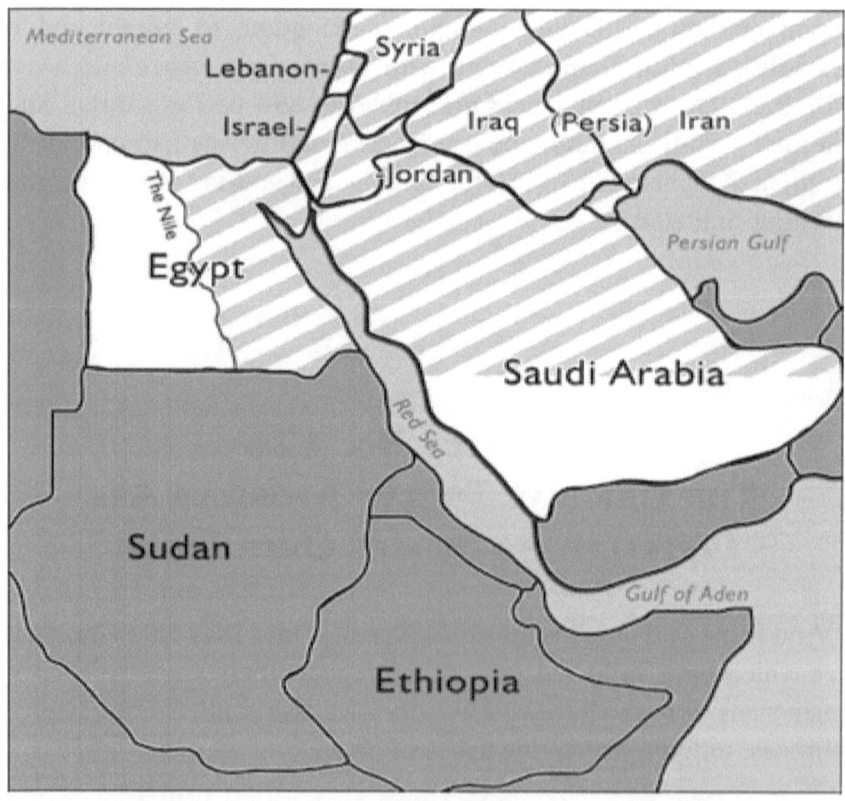

The Striped Land Shall be Annexed as New Israel at Christ's Second Coming and Egypt, Israel, Jordan, Saudi Arabia, Iraq (Ur), Iran, Syria, and Lebanon shall comprise New Israel.

PROPHECY NO. 128
ALL NATIONS TO SEND DELEGATES ANNUALLY TO THE FEAST OF TABERNACLES OR BE PUNISHED

"And it shall be, that whoso will not come up of all the families of the earth unto Jerusalem to worship the King, the LORD of hosts, even upon them shall be no rain. And if the family of Egypt go not up, and come not, that have no rain; there shall be the plague, wherewith the LORD will smite the heathen that come not up to keep the feast of tabernacles."

(Zechariah 14:17-18)

PROPHECY NO. 129
A COUP WILL TAKE PLACE AGAINST CHRIST'S RULE

"And when the thousand years are expired, Satan shall be loosed out of his prison, And shall go out to deceive the nations which are in the four quarters of the earth, Gog, and Magog [old European name for Russia], to gather them together to battle: the number of whom is as the sand of the sea. And they went up on the breadth of the earth, and compassed the camp of the saints about, and the beloved city [Jerusalem]: and fire came down from God out of heaven, and devoured them."

(Revelation 20:7-9)

PROPHECY NO. 130
THE DECEIVER TO BE CAST INTO
THE LAKE OF FIRE

"And the devil that deceived them was cast into the lake of fire and brimstone, where the beast and the false prophet are, and shall be tormented day and night for ever and ever."

(Revelation 20:10)

PROPHECY NO. 131
CHRIST HOLDS COURT

"For the Father judgeth no man, but hath committed all judgment unto the Son: That all men should honour the Son, even as they honour the Father. He that honoureth not the Son honoureth not the Father which hath sent him. Verily, verily, I say unto you, He that heareth my word, and believeth on him that sent me, hath everlasting life, and shall not come into condemnation... Verily, verily, I say unto you, The hour is coming, and now is, when the dead shall hear the voice of the Son of God: and they that hear shall live. For as the Father hath life in himself; so hath he given to the Son to have life in himself; And hath given him authority to execute judgment also, because he is the Son of man. Marvel not at this: for the hour is coming, in the which all that are in the graves shall hear his voice, And shall come forth; they that have done good, unto the resurrection of life; and they that have done evil, unto the resurrection of damnation... And the Father himself, which hath sent me, hath borne witness of me... And ye have not his word abiding in you: for whom he hath sent, him ye believe not. Search the scriptures; for in them ye think ye have eternal life: and they are they which testify of me. And ye will not come to me, that ye might have life."

(Jesus Christ, the Son of God - John 5:22-40)

- ✓ Hear O Israel the LORD our God is one LORD. (Deut. 6:4)

- ✓ Jesus Christ, the Son of God, stated, "I and my father are one." (John 10:30)

- ✓ "If you have seen me you have seen the father." (John 10:30)

- ✓ The last book of the Bible by its full title is called "The Revelation of Jesus Christ" revealing that He and the Father are one. The same one who stated, "Let Us [plural] make man in Our [plural] on image [singular]. "Hear O Israel the LORD thy God is one LORD." The revealed "one Lord" is the revelation of Lord Jesus Christ. (See: Did the God of Israel have a Son? What did the Jewish Prophets Say?)

Prophecy No. 132
The Great White Throne
Judgment Day

"And I saw a great white throne, and him that sat on it, from whose face the earth and the heaven fled away; and there was found no place for them. And I saw the dead, small and great, stand before God; and the books were opened: and another book was opened, which is the book of life: and the dead were judged out of those things which were written in the books, according to their works. And the sea gave up the dead which were in it; and death and hell delivered up the dead which were in them: and they were judged every man according to their works. And death and hell were cast into the lake of fire. This is the second death. And whosoever was not found written in the book of life was cast into the lake of fire."

(Revelation 20:11-15)

✓ "… he shall be tormented with fire and brimstone in the presence of the holy angels, and in the presence of the Lamb: And the smoke of their torment ascendeth up for ever and ever: and they have <u>no rest day nor night</u>…" (Revelation 14:10-11)

✓ "Because they rebelled against the words of God, and contemned the counsel of the most High: Therefore he brought down their heart with labour; they fell down, and there was none to help." (Psalms 107:11-12)

✓ "Behold, is it not of the LORD of hosts that the people shall <u>labour in the very fire</u>, and the people shall weary themselves for very vanity?" (The Prophet Habakkuk 2:13)

✓ "The wicked shall be turned into hell, and all the nations that forget God." (Psalm 9:17)

✓ Ministers who thought that placing faith in Christ was too easy to obtain the gift of eternal life, but rather used their good works to make Jesus their "Lord" will be cast into hell because eternal life is a gift by faith and not by works. Jesus Christ stated, "Many will say to me in that day, Lord, Lord, have we not prophesied [preached] in thy name? and in thy name have cast out devils? and in thy name done many wonderful works [good works]? And then will I profess unto them, I never knew you: depart from me, ye that work iniquity." (Matt. 7:22-23) Salvation is a gift by having faith in Jesus Christ, and not by doing good works for it. "Believe on the Lord Jesus Christ and thou shalt be saved," for by the works of keeping the laws of Moses shall no flesh living be justified. (Acts 16:31, Romans 3:20) Jesus prophesied, "Do not think that I will accuse you to the Father: there is one that accuseth you, even Moses, in whom ye trust. For had ye believed Moses, ye would have believed me; for he wrote of me. But if ye believe not his writings, how shall ye believe my words?" (John 5:45-47)

✓ "Believe on the Lord Jesus Christ and thou shalt be saved." (Acts 16:31) For the only unforgivable sin is not receiving forgiveness of sin coupled with life eternal by believing in Christ Jesus. Read our free book online <u>One Hundred Reasons Why Born Again Believers Cannot Lose their Salvation</u>: *Salvation by Grace Explained. Available free* at www.haveyouheardthegoodnews.org.

PROPHECY NO. 133
JESUS CHRIST ABDICATES EARTHLY THRONE IN JERUSALEM TO INSTALL DAVID AS ITS KING AS PROMISED

"And I will set up one shepherd over them and he shall feed them even my servant David; he shall feed them, and he shall be their shepherd. And I the LORD will be their God, and my servant David a prince among them; I the LORD have spoken it. And I will make with them a covenant of peace, and will cause the evil beasts to cease out of the land: and they shall dwell safely in the wilderness, and sleep in the woods. And I will make them and the places round about my hill a blessing; and I will cause the shower to come down in his season; there shall be showers of blessing. And the tree of the field shall yield her fruit, and the earth shall yield her increase, and they shall be safe in their land, and shall know that I am the LORD, when I have broken the bands of their yoke, and delivered them out of the hand of those that served themselves of them. And they shall no more be a prey to the heathen, neither shall the beast of the land devour them; but they shall dwell safely, and none shall make them afraid. And I will raise up for them a plant of renown, and they shall be no more consumed with hunger in the land, neither bear the shame of the heathen any more. Thus shall they know that I the LORD their God am with them, and that they, even the house of Israel, are my people, saith the Lord GOD. And ye my flock, the flock of my pasture, are men, and I am your God, saith the Lord GOD... They will live in the land I gave to my servant Jacob, the land where your fathers lived. They and their children and their children's children will live there forever, and David my servant will be their prince forever..."

(Ezekiel 34:23-31, 37:25)

PROPHECY NO. 134
THE DAY OF THE LORD COMES AS A THIEF IN THE NIGHT FOLLOWED BY THE DAY OF GOD

"But the **day of the Lord** [Christ's reign of a thousand years] will come as a thief in the night; in the which the heavens shall pass away with a great noise, and the elements [earth, water, fire, air] shall melt with fervent heat, the earth also and the works that are therein shall be burned up. Seeing then that all these things shall be dissolved, what manner of persons ought ye to be in all holy conversation [lifestyle] and godliness, Looking for and hasting unto the coming of the **day of God** [the rulership of God throughout eternity], wherein the heavens being on fire shall be dissolved, and the elements shall melt with fervent heat? Nevertheless we, according to his promise, look for new heavens and a new earth, wherein dwelleth righteousness."

(2 Peter 3:10-13)

PROPHECY NO. 135
LIFESPAN OF EARTH INHABITANTS INCREASED

"And I saw a new heaven and a new earth: for the first heaven and the first earth were passed away; and there was no more sea." (Revelation 21:1) " For, behold, I create new heavens and a new earth: and the former shall not be remembered, nor come into mind. But be ye glad and rejoice for ever in that which I create: for, behold,

I create Jerusalem a rejoicing, and her people a joy. And I will rejoice in Jerusalem, and joy in my people: and the voice of weeping shall be no more heard in her, nor the voice of crying. There shall be no more thence an infant of days, nor an old man that hath not filled his days: for the child shall die an hundred years old; but the sinner being an hundred years old shall be accursed."

(Isaiah 65:17-20)

- ✓ Under His reign of righteousness, one can live up to 100 years and then must submit to Christ as Lord or be accursed (put to death). Capital punishment will be on earth when Christ rules with "a rod of iron."

- ✓ Notice that death will exist for a time in the new heaven and the new earth.

PROPHECY NO. 136
CHRIST RESTORES HEAVEN & EARTH BACK TO HIS FATHER AS PERFECT
THE LAST ENEMY, DEATH IS DESTROYED

"Then cometh the end, when he shall have delivered up the kingdom to God, even the Father; when he shall have put down all rule and all authority and power. For he must reign, till he hath put all enemies under his feet. The last enemy that shall be destroyed is death....And when all things shall be subdued unto him, then shall the Son also himself be subject unto him that put all things under him, that God may be all in all."

(1 Corinthians 15: 24-28)

PROPHECY NO. 137
CHRIST REIGNS AS KING OF KINGS FROM NEW JERUSALEM

"And I saw a new heaven and a new earth: for the first heaven and the first earth were passed away; and there was no more sea. And I John saw the holy city, new Jerusalem, coming down from God out of heaven, prepared as a bride adorned for her husband. And I heard a great voice out of heaven saying, Behold, the tabernacle of God is with men, and he will dwell with them, and they shall be his people, and God himself shall be with them, and be their God. And God shall wipe away all tears from their eyes; and there shall be no more death, neither sorrow, nor crying, neither shall there be any more pain: for the former things are passed away. And he that sat upon the throne said, Behold, I make all things new. And he said unto me, Write: for these words are true and faithful."

(Revelation 21:1-5)

PROPHECY NO. 138
GOD'S PLAN FOR AGES TO COME

"That <u>in the ages to come</u> he might shew the exceeding riches of his grace in his kindness toward us through Christ Jesus.... To the intent that now unto the principalities and powers in heavenly places might be known by the church [the redeemed] the manifold wisdom of God."

(Ephesians 2:7, 3:10)

SECTION TEN

SIGNS OF HIS SECOND COMING

PROPHECY No. 139
WARNING SIGNS OF HIS SECOND COMING
A PARTY ATMOSPHERE PREVAILS PRIOR TO THE LORD'S RETURN

"Heaven and earth shall pass away but my words shall not pass away. And take heed to yourselves, lest at any time your hearts be overcharged with surfeiting [partying], and drunkenness, and cares of this life, and so that day come upon you unawares. For as a snare shall it come on all them that dwell on the face of the whole earth. Watch ye therefore, and pray always, that ye may be accounted worthy to escape all these things that shall come to pass, and to stand before the Son of man."

(Luke 21:33-36)

PROPHECY No. 140
CHURCH LEADERS DEPARTING FROM THE FAITH

"Now the Spirit speaketh expressly, that in the latter times some shall depart from the faith, giving heed to seducing spirits, and doctrines of devils."

(1 Timothy. 4:1)

- ✓ Church leadership involvement in ministry scandals

- ✓ Child molestation charges against trusted church ministers

- ✓ Church leaders departing from the faith to teach a universal salvation that everyone is going to heaven and there is no hell.

- ✓ Church leadership ordaining gay priests, which is against church doctrine

- ✓ Church leadership in sex scandals

- ✓ Church leadership performing gay marriages, which is against the teachings of Scripture

- ✓ Bibles, such as the New International Version (NIV) remove Satan's name "Lucifer" and insert Christ's title of "morning star" in its place without church protest. (Isa. 14:12, NIV)

- ✓ The only way books can be copyrighted is to be "significantly different" from the original manuscript and copyrighted Bibles are no different. Therefore, many new Bibles have subtly changed the doctrine that salvation is by grace through faith alone in Christ alone, to make salvation by humanitarianism (good works) plus God's grace, which is significantly different. (Romans 4:5)

PROPHECY NO. 141
WIDESPREAD BACKSLIDING BECOMES
COMMONPLACE IN THE CHURCH

"Let no man deceive you by any means: for that day shall not come, except there come a falling away first [Christians backsliding] ...."

(2 Thessalonians 2:3)

PROPHECY NO. 142
MANY WILL CLAIM TO BE CHRIST

"For many shall come in my name, saying, I am Christ; and shall deceive many."

(Matthew 24:5)

"...Take heed that ye be not deceived: for many shall come in my name, saying, I am Christ; and the time draweth near: go ye not therefore after them."

(Luke 21:8)

PROPHECY NO. 143
A PERFECT CONVERGENCE OF ALL SIGNS TO
MANIFEST IN ONE GENERATION

"So likewise ye, when ye shall see all these things, know that it is near, even at the doors. Verily I say unto you, This generation shall not pass till all these things be fulfilled."

(Matthew 24:33-34)

PROPHECY NO. 144
PERILOUS TIMES SHALL COME

"This know also, that in the last days perilous times shall come. For men shall be lovers of their own selves, covetous, boasters, proud, blasphemers, disobedient to parents, unthankful, unholy, Without natural affection, trucebreakers, false accusers, incontinent, fierce, despisers of those that are good, Traitors, heady, highminded, lovers of pleasures more than lovers of God; Having a form of godliness, but denying the power thereof: <u>from such turn away</u>. For of this sort are they which creep into houses, and lead captive silly women laden with sins, led away with divers lusts, Ever learning, and never able to come to the knowledge of the truth. Now as Jannes and Jambres withstood Moses, so do these also resist the truth: men of corrupt minds, reprobate concerning the faith. But they shall proceed no further: for their folly shall be manifest unto all men, as their's also was."

(Timothy 3:1-9)

✓ "For the wrath of God is revealed from heaven against all ungodliness and unrighteousness of men, who hold the truth in unrighteousness; Because that which may be known of God is manifest in them; for God hath shewed it unto them.... so that they are without excuse: Because that, when they knew God, they glorified him not as God, neither were thankful; but became vain in their imaginations, and their foolish heart was darkened. Professing themselves to be wise, they became fools, And changed the glory of the uncorruptible God into an image made like to corruptible man, and to birds, and fourfooted beasts, and creeping things. Wherefore God also gave them up to uncleanness through the lusts of their own hearts, to dishonour their own bodies between themselves: Who changed the truth of God into a lie, and worshipped and served the creature more than the Creator, who is blessed for ever. Amen. For this cause God gave them up unto vile affections: for even their women did change the natural use into that which is against nature: And likewise also the men, leaving the natural use of the woman, burned in their lust one toward another; men with men working that which is unseemly, and receiving in themselves that recompence of their error which was meet. And even as they did not like to retain God in their knowledge, God gave them over to a reprobate mind, to do those things which are not convenient; Being filled with all unrighteousness, fornication, wickedness, covetousness, maliciousness; full of envy, murder, debate, deceit, malignity; whisperers, Backbiters, haters of God, despiteful, proud, boasters, inventors of evil things, disobedient to parents, Without understanding, covenant breakers, without natural affection, implacable, unmerciful: Who knowing the judgment of God, that they which commit such things are worthy of death, not only do the same, but have pleasure in them that do them." (Romans 1:18-32)

✓ Scoffers and skeptics will begin mocking Christians who will begin proclaiming seven years, prematurely that Jesus is coming soon. Peter prophesied that many will say, "Where is the promise of his coming? for since the fathers fell asleep, all things continue as they were…" (2 Peter 3:4)

✓ According to Scripture, Jerusalem is the time-piece of the world, so "Pray for the peace of Jerusalem: they shall prosper that love thee." (Psalm 122:6)

✓ The opinion of the religious world will be "My Lord delayeth his coming…" (Matthew 24:48)

✓ While world opinion be, "The LORD will not do good, neither will he do evil." (The Prophet Zephaniah 1:12)

✓ At a time ye think not your Lord doth come. "What I say unto you I say unto you all. Watch!" (Mark 13:37)

PROPHECY No. 145
NO MAN KNOWS THE DAY NOR THE HOUR OF CHRIST'S RETURN

"…when ye shall see these things come to pass, know that it is nigh, even at the doors. Verily I say unto you, that this generation shall not pass, till all these things be done. Heaven and earth shall pass away: but my words shall not pass away. But of that day and that hour knoweth no man, no, not the angels which are in heaven, neither the Son, but the Father. Take ye heed, watch and pray: for ye know not when the time is."

(Mark 13:29-33)

PROPHECY No. 146
SIGNS OF THE TIMES

"…O ye hypocrites, ye can discern the face of the sky; but can ye not discern the signs of the times?"

(Matthew 16:3)

"And when these things begin to come to pass, then look up, and lift up your heads; for your redemption draweth nigh. …So likewise ye, when ye see these things come to pass, know ye that the kingdom of God is nigh at hand. ... And take heed to yourselves, … and so that day come upon you unawares. For as a snare shall it come on all them that dwell on the face of the whole earth."

(Luke 21:28-35)

PROPHECY No. 147
BECAUSE CRIME SHALL ABOUND THE LOVE OF MANY SHALL WAX COLD

"And many false prophets shall rise, and shall deceive many. And because iniquity shall abound, the love of many shall wax cold. But as the days of Noah were [when violence covered the earth], so shall also the coming of the Son of man be. For as in the days that were before the flood they were eating and drinking, marrying and giving in marriage, until the day that Noe entered into the ark, And knew not until the flood came, and took them all away; so shall also the coming of the Son of man be."

(Matthew 24:11-12, 37-39)

PROPHECY No. 148
HE WILL RETURN QUICKLY

"He was in the world and the world was made by him, and the world knew him not... He which testifieth these things saith, Surely I come quickly. Amen. Even so, come, Lord Jesus. The grace of our Lord Jesus Christ be with you all. Amen."

(John 1:10, Revelation 22:20-21)

WATCH!

"At a time ye think not your Lord doth come. "What I say unto you I say unto you all. Watch."

(Jesus Christ: Mark 13:37)

PROPHECY NO. 149
HOW TO ESCAPE THE WRATH TO COME

Jesus Christ indicated the nearness of the rapture when he stated, **"When these things begin to come to pass, then look up, for your redemption draweth nigh."** (Luke 21:28) You need a savior, the same one who warned you of all this. **NO OTHER RELIGION CAN NOR TRIES TO INFORM YOU OF THE FUTURE WITH THIS TYPE OF ACCURACY.** Only the Lord God can do this, and He had it written down thousands of years before He sent His only Son, Jesus Christ, into the world to save those who believe in Him. Since "confession is made unto salvation," to escape the wrath that is to come, you must "...confess with your mouth that Jesus is Lord, and believe in your heart that God raised Him from the dead, and thou shall be saved." (Romans 10:9-10) By repenting of your sin of unbelief in Christ as Savior, your faith in Christ is counted for righteousness, not your good deeds, great behavior, moral excellence, or keeping the commandments. If you try to stand before God by your integrity, morality, or character in other words your <u>self</u>-righteousness, then you make God a fool for having sent His Son to die for your sins for evidently you didn't need it. Your good works can never save you. Only belief in the death and resurrection of God's own Son does that "For God so loved the world that He gave his only Son that whosoever believes in him should not perish but have everlasting life." (John 3:16) If you refuse to believe this simple message, please keep this <u>Prophecy Checklist</u> handy. You will certainly need it during the Great Tribulation that is coming upon the earth. "But he that believeth not is condemned..." (John 3:18) "Believe on the Lord Jesus Christ (works of his death, blood, and resurrection for you) and thou shalt be saved..." (Acts 16:31) *It pleased God by the foolishness of preaching to save them that believe. For the preaching of the cross is to them that perish foolishness; but unto us which are saved it is the power of God."*

(1 Corinthians 1:21, 18) For salvation [eternal life] is to "him that worketh not (at being good enough to be saved), but believeth in him that justifieth the ungodly [that's you and I], his faith is counted for righteousness." (Romans 4:5) Salvation is for sinners! What must I do to get the Second Birth? "Ask and you shall receive." Simply pray, "I believe Jesus is Lord and God raised him from the dead. Come into my heart, Lord Jesus. I want to be saved. Amen." At this moment, you have experienced the new birth with the divine nature of Jesus Christ being born into your heart as your Savior as well as your sinless life before God. You now have been granted "eternal salvation, eternal redemption, and eternal life" according to God's promise. Although you cannot feel Him, touch Him, see Him or taste Him, you now have Christ's divine nature in you (your ticket to heaven) that cannot sin and will never leave or forsake you. However, you also still have the nature of sin, human nature, laced with its sinful habits. Your outward lifestyle has not been transformed. Transformation of lifestyle will be the result of your purposeful pursuit of spiritual growth in grace. (Titus 2:11-13) By praying this prayer in faith, you only received the gift of salvation which is the "free gift" of eternal life. You have not become a disciple of Jesus Christ until you commit to studying the Apostle Paul's and the other Apostles' "instructions in righteousness." To become Christ's disciple you must deny yourself, but to become saved takes only an act of your faith in what Christ has done for you in dying for your sins and rising again to pay for your gift of eternal life, eternal salvation, and eternal redemption. *"For God sent not his Son into the world to condemn the world; but that the world through him might be saved. He that believeth on him is not condemned; but he that believeth not is condemned already, because he hath not believeth in the name of the only begotten Son of God."* (John 3:16) "Whosoever calleth upon the name of the Lord shall be saved...for there is none other name under heaven given among men whereby we must be saved." (Acts 2:21, 4:12) Therefore, "Believe on the Lord Jesus Christ and thou shalt be saved."

(Acts 16:31)

For more information on the permanence of your eternal salvation *a free book* is available online titled <u>One Hundred Reasons Why Born Again Believers Cannot Lose Their Salvation</u> at WWW.HAVEYOUHEARDTHEGOODNEWS.COM

PROPHECY No. 150
THE RAPTURE OF THE CHURCH WILL TAKE PLACE BEFORE THIS GREAT TRIBULATION STRIKES EARTH

"I also will keep thee from the hour of temptation [tribulation], which shall come upon all the world, to try them that dwell upon the earth."

(Jesus Christ: Revelation 3:10)

"For God hath not appointed us to wrath [the Great Tribulation], but to obtain salvation by our Lord Jesus Christ."

(1 Thessalonians 5:9)

"…ye turned to God from idols to serve the living and true God; And to wait for his Son from heaven, whom he raised from the dead, even Jesus, which delivered us from the wrath to come [the time of Jacob's (Israel's) trouble]."

(1 Thessalonians 1:9-10)

"The blessed hope" that theologians call *the rapture* of the Church was prophesied by the Apostle Paul who wrote, "I would not have you to be ignorant, brethren, concerning them which are asleep, [dead] that ye sorrow not, even as others which have no hope. For if we believe that Jesus died and rose again, even so them also which sleep [died] in Jesus will God bring with him. For this we say unto you by the word of the Lord, that we which are alive and remain unto the coming of the Lord shall not prevent [precede] them which are asleep [dead]. For the Lord himself shall descend from heaven with a shout, with the voice of the archangel, and with the trump [trumpet] of God: and the dead in Christ shall rise first: Then we which are alive and remain shall be caught up together with them in the clouds, to meet the Lord in the air: and so shall we ever be with the Lord. Wherefore, comfort one another with these words."

(1 Thessalonians 4:13-18)

"Behold, I shew you a mystery; We shall not all sleep [die], but we shall all be changed, In a moment, in the twinkling of an eye, at the last trump: for the trumpet shall sound, and the dead shall be raised incorruptible, and we shall be changed. For this corruptible must put on incorruption, and this mortal must put on immortality."

(1 Corinthians 15:51-53)

PROPHECY NO. 151
AFTER THE RAPTURE ALL BELIEVERS MUST APPEAR BEFORE THE JUDGMENT SEAT OF CHRIST

"For we must all appear before the judgment seat of Christ; that every one may receive the things done in his body, according to that he hath done, whether it be good or bad. Every man's work shall be made manifest: for the day shall declare it, because it shall be revealed by fire; and the fire shall try every man's work of what sort it is. If any man's work abide which he hath built thereupon, he shall receive a reward. If any man's work shall be burned, he shall suffer loss: but he himself shall be saved; yet so as by fire."

(2 Corinthians 5:10, 1 Corinthians 3:13-15)

- ✓ The believer's lifetime sins have already been washed away by the blood of Christ. Only the works of the believers will be judged.

Prophecy No. 152
The Marriage Supper

"Let us be glad and rejoice, and give honour to him: for the marriage of the Lamb is come, and his wife [the church of believers in Christ] hath made herself ready. And to her was granted that she should be arrayed in fine linen clean and white:… the righteousness of saints. And he saith unto me, Write, Blessed are they which are called unto the marriage supper of the Lamb. And he saith unto me, These are the true sayings of God."

(Revelation 19:7-9)

Prophecy No. 153
Bridal Feast

"And I say unto you, That many shall come from the east and west, and shall sit down with Abraham, and Isaac, and Jacob, in the kingdom of heaven."

(Matthew 8:11)

Prophecy No. 154
Christ Will Receive Those He Redeemed To Himself

"In my Father's house are many mansions: if it were not so, I would have told <u>you</u>. I go to prepare a place for <u>you</u>. And if I go and prepare a place for <u>you</u>, I will come again [His Second Coming], and receive <u>you</u> unto myself; that where I am, there <u>ye</u> may be also…I am the way, the truth, and the life: no man cometh unto the Father, but by me."

(John 14:2, 3, 6)

Prophecy No. 155
The Last Words of Jesus Christ in the Book of The Revelation

"He which testifieth these things saith, Surely I come quickly. Amen. Even so, come, Lord Jesus."

(Revelation 22:20)

"But, beloved, be not ignorant of this one thing, that one day is with the Lord as a thousand years, and a thousand years as one day."

(2 Peter 3:8)

✓ In light of this, according to Christ's timetable it has only been *two days* to Him (but 2,000 years to us) since His crucifixion and resurrection. Therefore, to him, He is returning quickly for its only been two days since His first appearance.

✓ All these prophecies were predicted by Jewish men who foretold of a coming Jewish messiah who, like Joseph of the Old Testament would be rejected by his brethren, and, like Joseph, His name would become great among the Gentiles according to the Prophet Malachi. (Malachi 1:11) This is none other than the name of Jesus Christ, whom the Old Testament prophet Micah foretold would be born in Bethlehem. (Micah 5:2)

Prophecy No. 156
The Time Is At Hand...

"This is the revelation of Jesus Christ, which God gave to him, to show unto his servants things which must shortly come to pass.... Blessed is he that readeth, and they that hear the words of this prophecy, and keep those things which are written therein: for the time is at hand."

(Revelation 1:1, 3)

"Lord, who hath believed our Report?"
Isaiah 53:1

"Believe On The Lord Jesus Christ and thou shall be saved and thy household."
(Acts 16:31)

SECTION ELEVEN

THE BIBLICAL HISTORY OF IRAQ

The history of Iraq is found in the book of beginnings known as Genesis in Scripture. Elementary schools oftentimes teach Iraq's history in early civilization when it was called Mesopotamia which means "land between two rivers." This historic land has two of the oldest rivers known to man flowing through its borders, the Tigris and Euphrates rivers. (Genesis 2:14) These same rivers flowed through the garden of Eden when Iraq was known as Assyria (Asshuria) founded by Asshur a Semite/Shemite, according to the King James Version of the Bible. (Gen. 10:11) The land we know today as Iraq had additional names. It has been called various names throughout history such as Persia, Babylon, Media of the Medes, and Ur of the Chaldees.

UR OF THE CHALDEES = BABYLON = PERSIA=ASSYRIA=MEDIA

Iraq is the birthplace of the most famous man in the world, although western civilization and the Far East are almost totally ignorant of his importance to world history. The man's name was Abraham, the friend of God, and three major religions of the world trace their roots back to him. When Abraham was born in the district we call Iraq today but was called "Ur of the Chaldees" in his time. (Gen. 11:28) According to Boyd's Bible Dictionary, the word

121

Ur means region and the word *Chaldees* means demons. Hence, Abram, who later was renamed Abraham by God, was born in what is known as a "region of demons."

It is interesting that this mysterious place we know as Iraq was known in ancient times as Ur of the Chaldees i.e., a region of demons. God told Abram to remove himself from that land and go to a land that He would show him and Abram obeyed. When the Jewish descendants of Abraham were brought into this land as slaves, a young Jewish boy named Daniel was brought before the king of this region renamed Babylon. When Daniel was older, he went without food for twenty-one days in prayer to the God of the Israelites. (Dan. 10:3) On the twenty-first day, an angel appeared unto Daniel and informed him that he had to fight the demon principality assigned over this district called Persia, and it took him twenty-one days to fight with the assistance of Michael the Archangel to get Daniel the answer to his prayer. Daniel wrote that an angel appeared to him and stated:

> "Fear not, Daniel: for from the first day that thou didst set thine heart to understand, and to chasten thyself before thy God, thy words were heard, and I am come for thy words. But **the prince of the kingdom of Persia withstood me one and twenty days**: but, lo, **Michael, one of the chief princes, came to help me;** and I remained there with the kings of Persia. Now I am come to make thee understand <u>what shall befall thy people [Jews] in the latter days</u>: for yet the vision is for many days." (Daniel 10:12-14)

A demon principality, known as the *Prince of Persia* was resisting the angelic messenger that was sent from God with the answer to Daniel's prayer the first day he prayed. Ur of the Chaldees, then renamed the Kingdom of Persia, had an assigned demon to that region of demons to withstand God's messager and message.

PRESENT DAY IRAQ & THE BOTTOM OF THE EUPHRATES RIVER

Ironically, according to the Revelation of Jesus Christ, the last book in the Bible, God has chained four fallen angels (demons) in the bottom of the Euphrates River that flows through Iraq, and these fallen angels, i.e. demons, shall be released in the end times to slay one third of mankind on the face of the earth.

> "And the sixth angel sounded, and I heard a voice from the four horns of the golden altar which is before God, Saying to the sixth angel which had the trumpet, **Loose the four angels which are bound in the great river Euphrates. And the four angels were loosed, which were prepared for an hour, and a day, and a month, and a year, for to slay the third part of men.**" (Revelation 9:13-15)

Iraq, formerly called Ur of the Chaldees interpreted a *region of demons*, has at this present hour four fallen angels, i.e. demons, bound in the bottom of the Great River Euphrates "in chains under the darkness" for a preset day, month, year, and hour to be loosed to execute the judgment of the wrath of God to slay one third of unrepentant mankind from the face of the earth. (Jude 15) *Believe it or not!*

SECTION TWELVE

THE PROPHETIC FULFILLMENT OF GOD'S TIMETABLE

THE PROPHETIC FULFILLMENT OF JEWISH HOLIDAYS DECLARE GOD'S TIMETABLE

The Old Testament foreshadows or foretells events to be fulfilled in the New Testament. In the Old Testament, God commanded Israel to observe seven holy days, called holidays by gentiles in modern times. Through the exact observance of these specific Jewish holy days, God fulfilled Bible prophecy thousands of years later on the exact day. In these end times, God will demonstrate the fulfillment of these Jewish holidays with the climax of the Second Coming. Watch.

THE FIRST HOLY DAY: THE FEAST OF PASSOVER – INITIATED

This was the day that God commanded Moses to tell the Jews to observe forever. It is in celebration of the night that God commanded perfectly flawless lambs to be slain and the blood of the lambs to be placed on the doorpost of all the homes of Jewish slaves in North Africa (Egypt). God sent his death angel throughout the land of Egypt. When it saw the blood of the lamb on the doorpost, all parties

125

in that home were given immunity from the death angel's grasp that night and freed from slavery the next morning. Those who refused to apply the lamb's blood to the doorpost of their dwelling had the firstborn of the household slain that fateful night.

The Feast of Passover – Fulfilled

Two thousand years later, "the lamb of God that taketh away the sin of the world" appeared in the person of Jesus Christ. On the exact day of the Jewish feast of Passover, Jesus Christ, as the "lamb of God," was hung on a cross, crucified for the sins of the world that all who believe in their heart that His death, blood, and resurrection was payment enough for their lifetime sin-debt would be spared the second death, called eternal damnation and given eternal life. The Jewish Apostle Paul wrote that Christ, the King of the Jews, is our Passover lamb. (1 Corinthians 5:7) Christ died for the sins of the world on the same day as the observance of the Feast of Passover. (John 19:14) Our firstborn, human nature, is a slave of sin but when the "Son sets you free you shall be free indeed," by His divine nature born again in you, once His blood is applied to the doorpost of your heart.

The Second Holy Day:
The Feast of Unleavened Bread – Initiated

On the night that Jews were to eat the Passover Lamb, they were also to partake of the bread that had no leaven (yeast) in it - *unleavened bread*. They were commanded not to put yeast in their bread that night because they would not have time for it to *rise* before Pharaoh would drive them out of the land of Egypt. Jews, on this holiday, take the middle piece of bread and break it. The bread is flat as a wafer, and has many stripes and is pierced. Jews call it matzoth.

THE FEAST OF UNLEAVENED BREAD – FULFILLED

Two thousand years later, Jesus Christ was born in Bethlehem, a name that means house of bread. Later He began calling Himself the Bread of Life that came down from heaven.(John 6:31-36) Anyone who partakes of Him will have everlasting life. Leaven or yeast to the Jews is symbolic of sin's corruption. On the exact observance of this holiday, Jesus Christ, the bread of life, took the middle piece of bread and broke it uttering the fulfillment of this holiday's symbol saying, "This is my body which is broken for you." Christ's sinless broken body hung on the middle cross as our sin offering "wounded for our transgressions and bruised for our iniquities...with ... stripes..." (Isa. 53:5) As the Jews' matzoth bread has stripes all over it and is pierced, so the body of Christ was whipped with many stripes and pierced in his crucifixion for mankind. While in the tomb, as foretold by the Jew's King David, Christ's body did not see corruption [decay]. (Psalms 16:10) On the exact observance of this holiday, the body of Christ was lying sinless in the tomb, covered with stripes and pierced like unleavened bread. As leaven or yeast, which typifies sin, was not added to this type of bread, Christ, sinless body, the bread of life had not yet *risen* from the dead.

THE THIRD HOLY DAY:
THE FEAST OF FIRSTFRUITS – INITIATED

God said to Moses, "Speak unto the children of Israel, and say unto them, When ye be come into the land which I give unto you, and shall reap the harvest thereof, then ye shall bring a sheaf of the firstfruits of your harvest unto the priest: And he shall wave the sheaf before the LORD, to be accepted for you: on the morrow after the Sabbath the priest shall wave it." (Leviticus 23:10-11)

THE FEAST OF FIRSTFRUITS – FULFILLED

The third day in Scripture is always typical of resurrection, whether it was the third day of creation and the dry land appeared, or Jonah emerging from the belly of the whale on the third day, and this third Jewish holy day is no different. On the exact day of the observance of this Jewish Feast of Firstfruits, Jesus Christ rose from the dead, and became "the firstfruits of them that slept [had died]." (1st Corinthians 15:20) Jesus Christ was raised from the dead on observance of the day of the Feast of Firstfruits, the morning *after* the Sabbath (Saturday).

THE FOURTH HOLY DAY:
THE FEAST OF PENTECOST – INITIATED

This feast was declared to observe the day that the Ten Commandments of Moses' Law were given to the Jews at Mount Sinai and 3,000 people died.

THE FEAST OF PENTECOST – FULFILLED

Two thousand years later, on the exact observance of this feast called Pentecost, the church was born.

> "When the day of Pentecost was fully come, they were all with one accord in one place. And suddenly there came a sound from heaven as of a rushing mighty wind, and it filled all the house where they were sitting.... And they were filled with the holy Ghost, and began to speak with other tongues, as the Spirit gave them utterance. And ... devout men thought they were drunk with new wine... and Peter spake saying, "Whosoever shall call on the name of the Lord shall be saved. Ye men of Israel, hear these words, Jesus of Nazareth, a man approved of God among you by miracles, which God did by him in the midst of you, as ye yourselves know. Him, have you taken with wicked hands and crucified and slain. Whom God has raised up, having loosed him from death: because it was impossible for him to be held by it even as David said.... Therefore let all the

house of Israel know assuredly, that God has made the same Jesus, whom ye have crucified, both Lord and Christ. When they heard this they were pricked to their hearts, and asked, What must we do to be saved? Repent [of your unbelief and believe on Jesus Christ.] "Then they that gladly received his word were baptized and the same day 3,000 were added to the church." (Excerpts from Acts Chapter 2)

THE FIFTH HOLY DAY:
FEAST OF TRUMPETS – (ROSH HASHANAH) INITIATED:

This holiday is in observance of the Jewish New Year, Rosh Hashanah. In ancient times a Jewish priest would take a trumpet, called a Shofar, and blow it. At the sound of this primitive trumpet, the people would stop what they were doing and gather at the temple as one body of worshippers on this Feast of Trumpets. This feast is celebrated in the month of September or sometimes early October. Jews celebrate it as Rosh Hashanah.

THE FEAST OF TRUMPETS WILL BE FULFILLED

Although, "no man knows the day or the hour of the coming of the Lord," this is not the Coming of the Lord, but represents the coming blessed hope which theologians call rapture of the church, which is to occur on the observance of the Feast of Trumpets.

> "Behold, I shew you a mystery; We shall not all sleep, but we shall all be changed, In a moment, in the twinkling of an eye, at the last trump: for the trumpet shall sound, and the dead shall be raised incorruptible, and we shall be changed. For this corruptible must put on incorruption, and this mortal must put on immortality. So when this corruptible shall have put on incorruption, and this mortal shall have put on immortality, then shall be brought to pass

the saying that is written, Death is swallowed up in victory." (1 Corinthians 15:51-54)

"For the Lord Himself shall descend from heaven with a shout, with the voice of the archangel, and with the trump [trumpet] of God: and the dead in Christ shall rise first: Then we which are alive and remain shall be caught up together with them in the clouds, to meet the Lord in the air: and so shall we ever be with the Lord." (1 Thessalonians 4:16-17)

In keeping with the timetable of these literally God-given Jewish holidays, the fulfillment of the Trumpet Feast known as Rosh Hashanah, that being the blessed hope known as the rapture, will occur in the month of September or possibly early October during the Feast of Trumpets, although the year is clearly unknown, the Apostle Paul lets us know that we are not to be ignorant of "the times and the seasons" of the day of the Lord. (1 Thessalonians 5:1)

THE SIXTH HOLY DAY: THE DAY OF ATONEMENT – (YOM KIPPUR) INITIATED:

This was the day when the high priest of Israel went into the holy of holies to sprinkle lamb's blood on the Ark of the Covenant (as seen in the Raiders of the Lost Ark) to obtain forgiveness for the nation of Israel's sins for a full year. The priest had bells and pomegranates on his garment that made sounds in the holy of holies, which indicated that God had not struck him dead for the sins of the people. The sound of these joy bells indicated that God accepted the lamb's blood as atonement for the sins of Israel and all Israel was saved from His wrath for a year. The Jews call this day Yom Kippur.

THE FULFILLMENT OF THE DAY OF ATONEMENT

This holiday generally occurs in the month of October. This is the only Israeli holiday in Scripture that is not called a feast. Its prophetic fulfillment will be the Second Coming of Jesus Christ, when "all Israel shall be saved" from annihilation from the armies of the world that will surround her on orders of the Anti-Semite/ Antichrist, the global ruler from Persian region, today known as Iraq/Iran. (See Section Six: The Anti-Semite/Antichrist for more information). Although all of these God-designated Jewish holidays will be fulfilled on the exact day God established for their observance thousands of years ago, this particular day will not follow that established pattern because Jesus indicated that if it did no life would be spared alive on earth. Therefore, the days will be shortened so it can be fulfilled that no man will know the day or the hour of the coming of the Lord. (Matthew 25:13) Jesus said it this way, "Except those days should be shortened [by His coming], there should no flesh be saved; but for the elect's [Israel's] sake those days shall be shortened." (Matthew 24:22) (See Section Seven: The Coming of the Lord) On this day the Scripture will be literally fulfilled that "all Israel shall be saved," by the Lamb of God revealed from heaven, Jesus Christ. (Romans 11:26)

THE SEVENTH HOLY DAY:
THE FEAST OF TABERNACLES – (SUCCOTH / SUKKOTH)
INITIATED

This is the last holy day that God commanded the Jews to observe. This holy day, as well as the other seven, is observed by Jews to this day. This holy day is known as the Feast of Booths in Leviticus chapter 23:33-43 where God commanded the Jews to build booths and stay in them seven days to commemorate how their forefathers lived after being freed from slavery in North Africa, Egypt called in Scripture "the land of Ham," named after Noah's second son. (Psalms 105:25,27, 106:22)

THE FULFILLMENT OF THE FEAST OF TABERNACLES

After the Second Coming of Christ, this feast will be spectacularly fulfilled when God Himself makes His tabernacle among men. Regarding Christ, the Greek Bibles states, "The Word was God and the Word was made flesh and *tabernacled* among us." (John 1:2) This feast will be fulfilled when "the tabernacle of God is with men, and he will dwell with them, and they shall be his people, and God himself shall be with them, and be their God." (Revelation. 21:3) After Christ "throughly purges His floor," the floor in His Temple (called the Court of the Gentiles where Islam's Shrine of the Dome of the Rock sits), God will dwell in the same temple in Jerusalem where the Anti-Semite / Antichrist will have earlier declared himself God," and Jerusalem shall be the capital of the world and all nations shall flow up to it on the Feast of Tabernacles to honor God. Christ will decree that any nation that does not send delegates to Jerusalem on this holy day will have rain withheld from their land. (Zechariah. 14:17)

What must I do to be saved [receive eternal life and escape the wrath to come]? "…Believe on the Lord Jesus Christ, and thou shall be saved, and thy house.

(Acts 16:31)

DOES GOD HAVE A SON? WHAT JEWISH PROPHETS SAY

According to the writings of the Jewish prophet Daniel, when three Hebrew men were cast into a burning fiery furnace for not bowing to Nebuchadnezzar, King of Babylon [Iraq], the Iraqi king looked into the fire and exclaimed, "Did we not cast three men bound into the fire? I see four men loose, walking in the midst of the fire, and they have no hurt; and the form of the fourth is like the Son of God." (Daniel 3:25) In Proverbs of King Solomon, the wisest of all men, also believed that the God of Israel, whom his father King David worshipped and served, had a Son. For Proverbs 30:4 states, "Who hath ascended up into heaven, or descended? Who hath gathered the wind in his fist? Who hath bound the waters in a garment? Who hath established all the ends of the earth? What is his name, and what is his son's name." (Proverbs 30:4) Therefore, God having a Son should not be a foreign concept to Jewish people for Isaiah, another Jewish prophet, foretold: "The Lord himself shall give you a sign; behold, a virgin shall conceive, and bear a son, and thou shall call his name Immanuel [interpreted, God with us]." (Isaiah 7:4) To date this sign has only been given to the Jewish race by way of The Virgin Miriam, Mary in English. The Jewish prophet also prophesied "Unto us a child is born and unto us a son is given... and his name shall be called the mighty God, the Prince of Peace." (Isaiah 9:6) A son called "the mighty God"? The God of Israel declares that He is one, yet stated "Let Us make man in Our own image." The son born of the Jewish virgin declared, "I and my father are one." (John 10:30) Jesus Christ was the virgin born Son of God that was given to the nation of Israel as prophesied, and he fulfilled the prophecy of the Jewish messiah that was to be born in Bethlehem per the Jewish prophet Micah. (Micah 5:2) Many Jewish people do not realize that Jesus Christ was Jewish and lived in a pro-Jewish way according to the laws of Moses. "For God so loved the world that He gave His only begotten Son that whosoever believeth in him should not perish but have everlasting life." (John 3:16) "In the beginning was the word and the word was with God and the word was God. He was in the world and the world was made by him and the world knew him not." (John 1:1,9) This God, known in Scripture as The God of Israel, had scribes and prophets of His chosen Hebrew people write that He declares the end from the beginning, and this prophecy checklist is where you can clearly see that He, the invisible God, alone is the true and the living God, and that His Son shall return according to His word.

THE PROPHESIES WE HEARD IN CHURCH, WE NOW SEE ON TELEVISION. MANY PEOPLE HAVE IGNORED THEIR BIBLES TO THE POINT WHERE PROPHECIES ARE BEING FULFILLED BEFORE THEIR EYES AND THEY DON'T RECOGNIZE THEM. THE BIBLE IS THE **_ONLY_** BOOK THAT ACCURATELY FORETELLS HOW THINGS WILL END. NO OTHER RELIGION'S RELIGIOUS SCRIPTURES ATTEMPTS THIS. PROPHECY CHECKLIST WILL KEEP YOU INFORMED OF THE PROPHETIC EVENTS THAT ARE UNFOLDING AS TIME USHERS IN THE SECOND COMING OF THE LORD JESUS CHRIST!

"WHEN YOU SEE THESE THINGS BEGIN TO COME TO PASS, LOOK UP FOR YOUR REDEMPTION DRAWETH NIGH. HEAVEN AND EARTH SHALL PASS AWAY BUT MY WORDS SHALL NOT PASS AWAY."

Quotations of Jesus Christ in Luke 21:28, 33

ORDER THE BOOKS:

ONE HUNDRED REASONS WHY BORN AGAIN BELIEVERS CANNOT LOSE THEIR SALVATION

SEE COLORFUL PROPHECY PICTORIALS AT

www.prophecychecklist.com

Prophecy Finder Index

Section One:
Signs Of The Last Days "The Beginning Of Sorrows" 1
- ✓ Ground Zero: Israel to become a nation predicted
- ✓ Terrorism toward israelis predicted
- ✓ Great Earthquakes & Pandemics predicted
- ✓ Fierce Hurricanes predicted
- ✓ Information Age Prophesied
- ✓ Corporate Greed: The Rich Fraudulently Withholding wages from Laborers in the End Times
- ✓ Successful Gay Rights Movement predicted
- ✓ Jerusalem To Become A Millstone Around The Necks Of Her Allies
- ✓ The Gospel of the Kingdom is Spread Throughout the World
- ✓ The Second Coming of Jesus Christ is to be Mocked As Ridiculous in the Last Days

Section Two:
The West's War With the Leaders of Iraq (Medes) And Iran (Persia) Prophesied By Daniel 9

Section Three:
The Tribulation Period Begins.........................…....17
- ✓ The Tribulation Period Begins
- ✓ Jesus Christ Releases the Four Horsemen of the Apocalypse Upon the Earth
  - ➢ **The First Horsemen: The Anti-Semite / Antichrist**
- ✓ War is Unleashed Upon the Earth
  - ➢ **The Second Horsemen: War**
- ✓ Weapons of Mass Destruction Unleashed
- ✓ Nuclear War
- ✓ National Leaders Perplexed

- ✓ Terrorism Dismantled and The Words of National Leaders Prior to Nuclear Destruction
- ✓ Nuclear Carnage
- ✓ Dust From Nuclear Blast Blocks Sunlight
- ✓ Radiation Produces Baldness on All Heads & Earth Mourns
- ✓ Nuclear Winter Caused By Nuclear War
- ✓ Radiation Makes Certain Lands Uninhabitable
- ✓ The Most Terrible Famine in World History
  - ➤ **The Third Horsemen: Famine**
- ✓ Men Eating Their Own Flesh
- ✓ No Escape from Pestilences, War, or Famine And Money Will Be Worthless

Section Four:
Global Mass Destruction...25
- ✓ One Fourth Of The World's Population is Killed
  - ➤ **The Fourth Horsemen: Widespread Death & Destruction**
- ✓ Asteroids Spray Earth Causing Dust to Block Sun
- ✓ A Great Shaking Upon the Earth
- ✓ The Seventh Seal Opened
- ✓ Seven Trumpets of Judgment Sound and Earth's Atmosphere Destroys much Plant Life
- ✓ Asteroid Falls Into the Sea and One Third of all Sea Life Perishes
- ✓ One Third of the Earth's Water Supply is Contaminated
- ✓ Heart Attacks Brought on by Fear
- ✓ The Skies are Darkened
- ✓ Oxygen Supply Divinely Protected
- ✓ New Locust Life Forms Emerge
- ✓ Iraq Enters World Stage in End Times with 200 Million Man Army Marching Across Her Euphrates Riverbed
- ✓ Widespread Drug Abuse

SECTION FIVE:
THE SEVEN LAST PLAGUES...…........... 33
- ✓ THE SEVEN VIALS OF THE WRATH OF GOD POURED UPON THE EARTH
- ✓ MUCH SEA LIFE DESTROYED
- ✓ GLOBAL WARMING PEAKS
- ✓ PAINFUL SORES & DARKNESS THROUGHOUT THE EARTH
- ✓ ARMIES OF THE EAST SUMMONED TO ARMAGEDDON
- ✓ THE GREATEST EARTHQUAKE IN WORLD HISTORY
- ✓ SEVEN HORRORS YET TO BE REVEALED

SECTION SIX:
THE ANTI-SEMITE / ANTICHRIST..................................…........…......39
- ✓ THE DESTABILIZATION OF PERSIA (IRAN) BY THE WEST
- ✓ THE ANTI-SEMITE / ANTICHRIST WILL NOT KNOW HE IS THE ROD OF GOD'S ANGER
- ✓ THREE RULERS OF THE DESTABILIZED MIDDLE EAST REGION WILL COME TO POWER PRIOR TO THE RISE OF THE GREATEST ANTI-SEMITE EVER, KNOWN AS THE ANTICHRIST
- ✓ THE FIRST OF THE PERSIAN GULF'S LAST FOUR RULERS
- ✓ SECOND RULER OF PERSIAN GULF MARRIES A PRINCESS IN A PEACE AGREEMENT AND OFFSPRING TO WAGE WAR
- ✓ ARABIAN RULERS SHALL WAR OVER GULF REGION
- ✓ THE SECOND RULER OF PERSIAN GULF TO BE DEFEATED IN THE MIDST OF MANY YEARS OF GULF WARS
- ✓ THE THIRD GULF RULER RAISES TAXES TO RESTORE ITS INFRASTRUCTURE BUT WILL DIE OF NATURAL CAUSES
- ✓ THE BELIEF SYSTEM OF THE ANTI-SEMITE / ANTICHRIST
- ✓ THE ANTI-SEMITE / ANTICHRIST HONORS A STRANGE GOD
- ✓ THE ANTI-SEMITE / ANTICHRIST BRINGS PEACE COVENANT TO THE MIDDLE EAST
- ✓ SOLOMON'S TEMPLE TO BE REBUILT ON THE TEMPLE MOUNT
- ✓ THE ASSASSINATION OF THE ANTI-SEMITE / ANTICHRIST
- ✓ POST-RAPTURED POPE OF APOSTATE CHURCH ENCOURAGES WORSHIP OF THE ANTI-SEMITE / ANTICHRIST AFTER HIS "RESURRECTION"
- ✓ POST-RAPTURED POPE CALLED, THE FALSE PROPHET, COMMANDS A STATUE BE MADE FOR THE ANTI-SEMITE/ ANTICHRIST AFTER AN ASSASSINATION ATTEMPT

- ✓ THE FALSE PROPHET COMMANDS ALL NATIONS TO WORSHIP THE STATUE OF THE ANTI-SEMITE/ANTICHRIST OR BE EXECUTED
- ✓ THE FALSE PROPHET MANDATES THAT ALL PLEDGE ALLEGIANCE TO THE ANTI-SEMITE/ANTICHRIST BY TAKING THE "MARK"
- ✓ ALL THE ARMIES OF THE EARTH TO SURROUND JERUSALEM AND HER ENEMIES REJOICE
- ✓ JEWS WARNED TO FLEE JERUSALEM WHEN THE ANTI-SEMITE/ ANTICHRIST INVADES THEIR YET-TO-BE REBUILT JEWISH TEMPLE ON THE TEMPLE MOUNT
- ✓ THE ANTI-SEMITE/ANTICHRIST ENTER THE ISRAELIS' TEMPLE STATING HE IS GOD
- ✓ THE TEMPLE IS DEFILED BY THE ANTI-SEMITE / ANTICHRIST
- ✓ THE ANTI-SEMITE/ANTICHRIST CURSES GOD ALMIGHTY AFTER DECLARING HIMSELF TO BE GOD
- ✓ THE ANTI-SEMITE/ANTICHRIST CURSES THE RAPTURED AND DECEASED SAINTS IN HEAVEN
- ✓ THE ANTI-SEMITE/ANTICHRIST DECLARES WAR ON THE SAINTS OF GOD
- ✓ THE ANTI-SEMITE/ANTICHRIST BLASPHEMES GOD AND CRUSHES BELIEVERS
- ✓ THE ANTI-SEMITE/ANTICHRIST WILL BE REVERED
- ✓ THE ANTI-SEMITE/ANTICHRIST GOES FORTH TO CONQUER
- ✓ RUSSIA WARS AGAINST THE ANTI-SEMITE / ANTICHRIST
- ✓ THE ANTI-SEMITE/ANTICHRIST DEVASTATES EGYPT
- ✓ THE ANTI-SEMITE /ANTICHRIST ENJOYS THE SPOILS OF WAR AND PRACTICES SOCIALISM IN REDISTRIBUTING WEALTH
- ✓ THE PEACE COVENANT WITH ISRAEL IS BROKEN
- ✓ JERUSALEM IS INVADED
- ✓ A DIVIDED JERUSALEM TO BE PLUNDERED
- ✓ JERUSALEM UNDER SIEGE BY THE ANTI-SEMITE / ANTICHRIST MAN-MADE FAMINE SPAWNS CANNIBALISM
- ✓ TWO-THIRDS OF JEWS MASSACRED BY THE ANTI-SEMITE / ANTICHRIST, AS ISRAEL LOOKS IN VAIN FOR AMERICA TO RESCUE HER; ONLY ONE-THIRD OF THE JEWISH POPULATION IN THE LAND OF ISRAEL WILL SURVIVE
- ✓ THE WORLD IS ASTONISHED AT THE INVASION OF ISRAEL AND THE SIEGE OF JERUSALEM
- ✓ THE ANTI-SEMITE/ANTICHRIST IS CALLED A DESTROYER OF THE GENTILES [A TERM FOR EUROPEANS IN SCRIPTURE]

- ✓ 144,000 Jewish Men Ordained by God to Preach the Gospel of the Kingdom During the Tribulation
- ✓ The Gospel of the Kingdom is Preached to All The World then Shall the End Come
- ✓ God Commissions Two Witnesses to Earth
- ✓ Worldwide Media Covers the Deaths of the Two Witnesses
- ✓ Believers Will Be Betrayed to the State by Family Members
- ✓ The Anti-Semite/Antichrist Will Behead Preachers of the Gospel of Christ's Return, the Gospel of the Kingdom
- ✓ The Anti-Semite/Antichrist Makes War Against God's Saints
- ✓ God Avenges His Martyred Saints
- ✓ Martyred Saints Receive White Robes from God
- ✓ Post-Raptured Catholic Church of Rome is Judged
- ✓ The Anti-Semite / Antichrist Attacks Vatican City
- ✓ The Stage is Set for the Great Battle of Armageddon

Section Seven:
The Coming Of The Lord 77
- ✓ The Lord Assembles His Mighty Army to Invade Earth
- ✓ Jesus Christ Returns
- ✓ The Second Coming of Jesus Christ
- ✓ The Earth Laments Christ's Return
- ✓ All Tribes of the Earth Mourn Christ's Return
- ✓ Every Eye on Earth Shall See His Second Coming
- ✓ Kings of the Earth Make War Against Christ at His Return
- ✓ The Lord Takes Vengeance on Unbelievers
- ✓ The Battle of Armageddon, Christ Massacres Earth's Armies
- ✓ The Lord Will Fight for Jerusalem
- ✓ The Lord Destroys Those Who Fought Against Jerusalem
- ✓ The Lord Utters His Mighty Voice Before His Army and His Saints Execute Judgment
- ✓ Jesus Christ Smites the Nations
- ✓ Christ Slays the Armies Gathered at Armageddon

- ✓ THE BLOOD OF THE 200 MILLION MAN ARMIES, SLAIN BY CHRIST AT ARMAGEDDON, WILL BE MORE THAN THREE FEET DEEP AND COVER OVER 100 MILES
- ✓ CHRIST PUTS DOWN THE ANTI-SEMITE / ANTICHRIST & WATERS THE BATTLEFIELD WITH THE BLOOD OF EARTH'S ARMIES
- ✓ THE ANTI-SEMITE / ANTICHRIST'S POWER IS BROKEN

SECTION EIGHT:
THE DAY OF THE LORD...87
- ✓ THE KINGS OF THE EARTH ARE PUNISHED
- ✓ THE DAY OF THE LORD
- ✓ CHRIST REVEALS THE WOUNDS FROM HIS CRUCIFIXION TO THE JEWISH SURVIVORS OF THE ANTI-SEMITE / ANTICHRIST SIEGE
- ✓ JEWISH SURVIVORS OF THE TRIBULATION MOURN THE SINS OF THEIR FOREFATHERS' CRUCIFIXION OF JESUS CHRIST

SECTION NINE:
CHRIST'S MILLENNIAL REIGN.............................91
- ✓ THE MILLENNIAL (THOUSAND YEAR) REIGN OF JESUS CHRIST BEGINS
- ✓ SATAN IS BOUND FOR A THOUSAND YEARS AND CAST INTO THE BOTTOMLESS PIT
- ✓ SATAN MOCKED BY WORLD LEADERS ALREADY IN HELL AS HE DESCENDS INTO ITS PIT
- ✓ CHRIST ESTABLISHES JERUSALEM AS THE CAPITOL OF THE WORLD
- ✓ JERUSALEM FINALLY AT PEACE
- ✓ THE HOUSE OF THE LORD SHALL BE ESTABLISHED
- ✓ CHRIST BRINGS TRUE PEACE TO THE MIDDLE EAST
- ✓ A HIGHWAY OUT OF EGYPT IS TO BE BUILT
- ✓ PEACE ON EARTH THE LION WILL LIE DOWN IN PEACE WITH THE LAMB
- ✓ ISRAEL TO BE COMFORTED BY HER KING
- ✓ JESUS CHRIST REIGNS IN JERUSALEM AS KING OF KINGS AND LORD OF LORDS
- ✓ THE ORIGINAL TWELVE APOSTLES ARE INSTALLED AS JUDGES OVER ISRAEL

- ✓ Christ Annexes Vast Amounts of Land in the Mid-East as New Israel to Fulfill God's Old Testament Promise to, His Chosen People, The Jews
- ✓ All Nations to Send Delegates Annually to the Feast of Tabernacles or be Punished
- ✓ A Coup Will Take Place Against Christ's Rule
- ✓ The Deceiver To Be Cast Into the Lake of Fire
- ✓ Christ Holds Court
- ✓ The Great White Throne: Judgment Day
- ✓ Jesus Christ Abdicates Earthly Throne in Jerusalem to Install David as King of Jerusalem as Promised
- ✓ The Day of the Lord Comes as a Thief in the Night followed by the day of God
- ✓ Lifespan of Earth's Inhabitants Increased
- ✓ Christ Restores Heaven & Earth Back to His Father as Perfect and the Last Enemy Death is Destroyed
- ✓ Christ Reigns as King of Kings from New Jerusalem
- ✓ God's Plan for Ages to Come

Section Ten:
Signs of His Second Coming………..…………………………107

- ✓ Warning Signs Of His Second Coming A Party Atmosphere Prevails Prior to the Lord's Return
- ✓ Church Leaders Departing From the Faith
- ✓ Widespread Backsliding Becomes Commonplace in the Church
- ✓ Many Will Claim to be Christ
- ✓ A Perfect Convergence of All Signs to Manifest in One Generation
- ✓ Perilous Times Shall Come
- ✓ No Man Knows the Day or the Hour of Christ's Return
- ✓ Signs of the Times
- ✓ Because crime shall abound The Love of Many Shall Wax Cold
- ✓ He Will Return Quickly
- ✓ Watch!
- ✓ How To Escape The Wrath To Come
- ✓ The Rapture of the Church Will Take Place Before the Great Tribulation Strikes Earth

- ✓ After the Rapture, All Believers Must Appear Before the Judgment Seat of Christ
- ✓ The Marriage Supper
- ✓ Bridal feast
- ✓ Christ Will Receive Those He Redeemed To Himself
- ✓ The Last Words of Jesus Christ in the Book of the Revelation
- ✓ The Time is at Hand...

Section Eleven:
The Biblical History of Iraq......................................121

Section Twelve:
The Prophetic Fulfillment of God's Timetable Through Jewish Feast 125
- ✓ Feast Of Passover
- ✓ Feast Of Unleavened Bread
- ✓ Feast Of First Fruits
- ✓ Feast Of Pentecost
- ✓ Feast Of Trumpets
- ✓ Day Of Atonement

Feast Of Tabernacles..131

FREE BOOK ONLINE

By belief in Christ for eternal salvation your faith was exchanged for His eternal righteousness. For more information on the permanence of your eternal salvation another **FREE BOOK ONE HUNDRED REASONS WHY BORN AGAIN BELIEVERS CANNOT LOSE THEIR SALVATION** is online at www. haveyouheardthegoodnews.com

For additional copies of this book order online:
www.prophecychecklist.com or
www.haveyouheardthegoodnews.org